Proverbs for Recovery

Also by Barbara Stephens
Psalms for Recovery

Proverbs for Recovery

MEDITATIONS FOR STRENGTH AND WISDOM

Barbara Stephens

HarperSanFrancisco
A Division of HarperCollins*Publishers*

PROVERBS FOR RECOVERY: *Meditations for Strength and Wisdom.* Copyright © 1992 by Barbara Stephens. All rights reserved. Printed in the United States of America. No part of this book may be used or reproduced in any manner whatsoever without written permission except in the case of brief quotations embodied in critical articles and reviews. For information address HarperCollins Publishers, 10 East 53rd Street, New York, NY 10022.

FIRST EDITION

Library of Congress
Cataloging-in-Publication Data

Stephens, Barbara.
    Proverbs for recovery : meditations for strength and wisdom / Barbara Stephens. — 1st ed.
        p.   cm.
    ISBN 0–06–067593–4 (alk. paper)
    1. Bible. O.T. Proverbs—Meditations. 2. Twelve-step programs—Religious aspects—Christianity—Meditations. I. Title.
    BS1465.4.S74 1992
    242′.4—dc20

91–58177
CIP

92 93 94 95 96 ❖ K.P. 10 9 8 7 6 5 4 3 2 1

This edition is printed on acid-free paper that meets the American National Standards Institute Z39.48 Standard.

Introduction

Recovery began when we realized that we could not numb enough pain and continue to live, that we were merely existing. The early stages of recovery—getting clean, learning to process the avalanche of awakening emotions, and beginning to practice the Steps—were actually our baby steps in a lifetime of recovery.

Many people begin the journey but fail to grow up. They often no longer use their drugs of choice (alcohol, drugs, relationships, spending, tobacco, food, gambling), but the addictive personality has not undergone change. *Proverbs for Recovery* takes the recovering person deeper into the journey, looking squarely at the attitudes that hinder our recovery. Whether we have been on the journey for a month or a few years, *Proverbs for Recovery* helps bring us into the maturity needed to maintain our life-style of recovery.

The Twelve Steps

1. We admitted we were powerless over [addiction], that our lives had become unmanageable.

2. Came to believe that a Power greater than ourselves could restore us to sanity.

3. Made a decision to turn our will and our lives over to the care of God *as we understood Him.*

4. Made a searching and fearless moral inventory of ourselves.

5. Admitted to God, to ourselves, and to another human being the exact nature of our wrongs.

6. Were entirely ready to have God remove all these defects of character.

7. Humbly asked Him to remove our shortcomings.

8. Made a list of all persons we had harmed, and became willing to make amends to them all.

9. Made direct amends to such people wherever possible, except when to do so would injure them or others.

10. Continued to take personal inventory and, when we were wrong, promptly admitted it.

11. Sought through prayer and meditation to improve our conscious contact with God, *as we understood Him,* praying only for knowledge of God's will for us and the power to carry that out.

12. Having had a spiritual awakening as the result of these steps, we tried to carry this message to [others] and to practice these principles in all our affairs.

Being "clean," free from my codependent relationships, brought me into full awareness that much was lacking in my character and personality. The early steps that started my recovery had uncovered work to be done, attitudes and behavior to be corrected. Much like a baby who had been weaned but then grabbed for her thumb and security blanket, I found that I could become obsessive about other things. Now came the lifelong process of maturing in my Twelve-Step living. The wisdom of Proverbs became my schoolmaster in the daily details of recovery. The Book of Proverbs confronted me with myself, areas lacking discipline and needing strength, relationship weaknesses, and gave me the needed instruction to further develop my recovery.

—B.S.

Proverbs 1: 1–6

The proverbs of Solomon, son of David, king of Israel: for attaining wisdom and discipline; for understanding words of insight; for acquiring a disciplined and prudent life, for doing what is right and just and fair; for giving prudence to the simple, knowledge and discretion to the young— let the wise listen and add to their learning, and let the discerning get guidance—for understanding proverbs and parables, the sayings and riddles of the wise.

In reading the Proverbs, we might wonder if Solomon was in some kind of Twelve-Step program. His wisdom and insight into all areas of life bring maturity to our earlier steps of recovery.

The first six verses give us the reasons Solomon wrote the Proverbs. They are not just cute riddles, paradoxes, or allegories. They are words of affirmation, strength, and wisdom that develop our recovery into adult steps, stable and secure. The Proverbs help us to

- attain wisdom and discipline
- understand words of insight
- acquire a disciplined and prudent life
- do what is right and just and fair
- gain knowledge and discretion.

If we are wise, we can listen and add to our knowledge. We can learn to discern, and we can accept guidance. We all need the wisdom and affirmation that Proverbs can add to our recovery. Our recovery began with faltering and unstable childlike steps. Proverbs adds stability and trains us to walk as recovering adults.

Lord, teach me how to grow up in my recovery.

Proverbs 1: 7–9

The fear of the Lord is the beginning of knowledge, but fools despise wisdom and discipline. Listen, my son, to your father's instruction, and do not forsake your mother's teaching. They will be a garland to grace your head and a chain to adorn your neck.

"God, as we understand him," is a comforting and welcoming term for those who have not been acquainted with God or those who have been hurt by religion. Our understanding of God can grow, mature, and develop as we continue improving our conscious contact with God through prayer and meditation. Our recovery will grow as we grow in our knowledge of God. Our sponsors, our spiritual mothers and fathers, others who are actively recovering can encourage our concept of God. Their wisdom, instruction, and teaching can help us stretch past what was once comfortable.

Until we are able to better know the Lord, our recovery will lack the power only God can give. When our recovery is attempted in our own strength, we are bound to falter. Only God can remove the old patterns we have ingrained into the broken places in our heart. As we come to know him better, we can trust him to change us from the inside out. What a marvelous change he brings about as we rest in his love. Truly this wisdom becomes a garland that graces our heads and a chain to adorn our necks.

O God, help my understanding of you to grow each day.

Proverbs 1: 20–23

Wisdom calls aloud in the street, she raises her voice in the public squares; at the head of the noisy streets she cries out, in the gateways of the city she makes her speech. How long will you simple ones love your simple ways? How long will mockers delight in mockery and fools hate knowledge? If you had responded to my rebuke, I would have poured out my heart to you and made my thoughts known to you.

In recovery we come to hate the ways of addiction/codependency before we become thankful for what has been accomplished. We no longer fool ourselves into thinking that there is anything good in the old life-style. We no longer hold onto it, at least not consciously. As we stop loving the old life-style, we are able to abandon it.

When the ways of recovery become too difficult, we know there is no turning back. We've traveled much too far.

Wisdom in recovery was realizing that there is nothing good in addiction/codependency. Wisdom came as pain and disappointment; pressure and suffering turned knowledge into the ability to truly understand life. Wisdom has once and for all removed the blinders of rationalization and minimizing and

helped us face reality with honesty. Wisdom understands the need to make amends and takes on the
task. Recovery may be another word for wisdom.

*Father, help me continue to hate the ways of
addiction/codependency and love the ways of wisdom.*

Proverbs 2: 6–15

For the Lord gives wisdom, and from his mouth come knowledge and understanding. He holds victory in store for the upright, he is a shield to those whose walk is blameless, for he guards the course of the just and protects the way of his faithful ones. Then you will understand what is right and just and fair—every good path. For wisdom will enter your heart, and knowledge will be pleasant to your soul. Discretion will protect you, and understanding will guard you. Wisdom will save you from the ways of wicked men, from men whose words are perverse, who leave the straight paths to walk in dark ways, who delight in doing wrong and rejoice in the perverseness of evil, whose paths are crooked and who are devious in their ways.

There will always be people who start out on the road to recovery then decide to turn back. There will be people who have years of clean time who decide that recovery is not all it's cracked up to be. Once more they will fall into the addiction/codependency life-style. How can we keep from becoming people who fail to continue recovery? This proverb invites us to come to the God of the Second Step. He gives us wisdom, knowledge, and understanding. He becomes a shield to protect and guard our recovery; therefore, we can experience daily victory. The wisdom that he gives every day saves us from returning to the path of addiction/codependency. Our God did restore us, and, as we continue to turn to him over and over, day by day, he continues that restoration. We continue to make those steps in the pathway that God provides for us, and we continue to grow and mature in our understanding of God and of our recovery.

O, God, help me turn to you when I feel myself slipping back.

Proverbs 3: 1–6

My son, do not forget my teaching, but keep my commands in your heart, for they will prolong your life many years and bring you prosperity. Let love and faithfulness never leave you; bind them around your neck, write them on the tablet of your heart. Then you will win favor and a good name in the sight of God and man. Trust in the Lord with all your heart and lean not on your own understanding; in all your ways acknowledge him, and he will make your paths straight.

Keeping the commands in Proverbs assures us of maturing steps in our recovery. Mature steps are required when the going gets tough and the journey becomes tiring. How easy it would be just to slide back into addiction/codependency. To prevent this from happening, we must remind ourselves of Solomon's teachings on a daily basis and take those corresponding steps to recovery. To do so will prolong our lives and bring prosperity.

Love and faithfulness bring us favor and a good name in God's sight as well as humankind's sight. We need love and the ability to stick to our recovery, to be faithful to ourselves, to God, and to significant people. To make it all come together, we see Steps Two and Three plainly as Solomon exhorts us to trust in the Lord completely and not to try to figure out in our minds this thing called recovery. Only God can bring us to wholeness, and only he can make our lives and pathways straight. Daily we rehearse the Steps, the proverbs, and the teachings. We choose to be faithful and to walk in love, and

then we choose to trust in the Lord, not to analyze,
and to constantly turn to the God of recovery.

*O God, help me be willing to grow up and take the
mature steps I'd rather avoid.*

Proverbs 3: 7–8

*Do not be wise in your own eyes, fear the Lord
and shun evil. This will bring health to your
body and nourishment to your bones.*

Many of our downfalls in recovery come about because we think we know everything. We get too big for our britches. When we think we're wise, we presume we have power because we have knowledge. How foolish to think we can outwit addiction/co-dependency by our puny human reasoning or knowledge. We are still powerless over addiction/codependency—that is true wisdom. Reverence the Lord, acknowledge him, honor and respect him as the only true God. He is, after all, the God of recovery. We must consciously make a decision and purpose in our hearts to recover and then depend on the strength of the Lord to take us through to victory. To walk away from temptation, to deny the old appetites, to be strong enough to say no, requires a strength far greater than ours. All of the meetings in the world can't help us until we have decided within ourselves to shun and avoid temptation. When we have made the decision, he is always there. The result of all this is new health and strength.

*O God, remind me that I'm often a know-it-all who
knows nothing at all.*

Proverbs 3: 9–10

*Honor the Lord with your wealth, with the
firstfruits of all your crops, then your barns will
be filled to overflowing, and your vats will brim
over with new wine.*

One of the places we suffer most is in our finances.
Our addiction/codependency has wounded our
budgets. We may have two jobs, but still we can't
make ends meet or even come within shouting distance of each other.

Solomon has a key to our finances, but many of
us don't like the key, and we keep on doing things
our way. To honor the Lord with our wealth, we acknowledge that he is the source of our ability to
make money; we have a grateful heart for his pro-
vision; we give to God what he has asked us for, and
then we use wisely that which we have left. We
honor God by the way we handle money. Many of
us need to develop skill in this area, but it is entirely possible to see our finances recover as we become wise in handling them. Recovery is the
doorway to health in every area of our lives—not
just in dependency on something or someone. God
gave us the plan of recovery, and it is no wonder
that he desires our finances to prosper as our emotions, spirits, and bodies recover. His blessings
never stop.

*O God, teach me the secret of handling the money you
have entrusted to me.*

Proverbs 3: 11–12

*My son, do not despise the Lord's discipline
and do not resent his rebuke, because the Lord
disciplines those he loves, as a father the son he
delights in.*

The longer we walk in recovery, the more we come
to understand the way of discipline in our lives.
The Twelve Steps brought needed discipline into
our lives to get us on the road of healing. As we
have matured in our understanding of recovery
and the need for discipline, we have become more
willing to have our heavenly Father correct us. For
many of us, to be corrected meant that we were bad
people, and discipline meant we were being rejected. Today we realize that our disease was bad,
our old nature is bad, but God's love and his plan to
change us from the inside develops good, strong
character. As we discipline our children because
we love them and want them to be the best they can
be, our Father corrects us and shapes us through
the wisdom found in Proverbs and the daily steps
of our recovery program.

God has a plan that will bring us to maturity and
health, and sometimes we will hear his loving rebuke. Our Father delights in us even though we are
deeply flawed and have far to go before we are
completely changed; he patiently continues, knowing that one day he will see his image in us.

*God, sometimes I feel like a naughty child when you
discipline me. Help me always to feel your love when
I'm being rebuked.*

Proverbs 3: 21–24

*My son, preserve sound judgment and
discernment, do not let them out of your sight;
they will be life for you, an ornament to grace our
neck. Then you will go on your way in safety,
and your foot will not stumble; when you lie
down, you will not be afraid; when you lie down,
your sleep will be sweet.*

As recovering people, we begin to develop sound
judgment and the ability to discern. Because our ad-
diction/codependency robbed us of soundness of
mind, we could not properly discern or judge.
Recovery begins to restore what we had lost, and
they become lovely ornaments attesting to the grace
of God in our lives.

His grace has changed us so much that we can
travel on our way knowing he will keep us safe. His
grace in our recovery will make our steps steadier.
One of the fringe benefits of recovery is that we
begin to enjoy times of rest from fear and anxious
thoughts. Holding onto sound judgment and discernment in the midst of stormy and rocky places
seems difficult at best, but if we continue to call out
to God for help and continue to reach out to others
in recovery, we will be able to make wise decisions.

Lord, thank you for the ability to judge wisely.

Proverbs 3: 25–26

Have no fear of sudden disaster or of the ruin that overtakes the wicked, for the Lord will be your confidence and will keep your foot from being snared.

The God of recovery is our reason for being confident. In our own power we will fail, but we will succeed if we allow the Lord to be our confidence. Relapse doesn't have to happen to any of us if we continue our complete dependence on God. We are free from the disaster and the ruin that once controlled and dominated us. God keeps our feet from being caught in the trap as we follow where he leads in recovery. Confidently we place our feet in the footprints God leaves, knowing that he knows the way through the wilderness. Our God will give us clear direction around the slippery people, places, and circumstances of our lives. As we continue to follow him, no disaster or ruin can overtake us. Following our own road map only left us in a mess, in confusion and turmoil.

Often we need to return to the Second and Third Steps, turning our lives and wills over to the care of God. Minute by minute we have to rely on him and his wisdom, because he alone knows where our weak places are and how easily we can become ensnared again. He is our confidence.

O God, help me place as much trust in you as I have placed in myself.

Proverbs 3: 27–28

Do not withhold good from those who deserve it,
when it is in your power to act. Do not say to
your neighbor, "Come back later; I'll give it
tomorrow"—when you now have it with you.

Control is a strong force in the lives of those of us
who are recovering from addiction/codependency.
It was trying to be in control of the disease that kept
us in bondage. We have also tried to control others,
sometimes by withholding blessing from people in
our lives. When we have the power to act and bless
someone who deserves it, we have a sense of control. Recovery and the wisdom of Solomon tell us
to give blessings freely.

Another way of being in control is to manipulate others who need something from us by delay-
ing or stalling. This is also an unhealthy way of
responding to those who need us. These are old
ways of control, and they no longer fit with our maturing steps of recovery. It becomes less and less
frightening to give over our need to be in control as
we become wiser in our Twelve-Step living. We become better able to give people the love and respect
they need rather than trying to have power over
them through control and manipulation. Our relationships truly will blossom under the freedom we
experience.

Lord, you are the only one who is wise enough
to control, and you don't force or
manipulate anyone

Proverbs 4: 7–12

*"Wisdom is supreme; therefore get wisdom.
Though it cost all you have, get understanding.
Esteem her, and she will exalt you; embrace her,
and she will honor you. She will set a garland of
grace on your head and present you with a crown
of splendor." Listen, my son, accept what I say,
and the years of your life will be many. I guide
you in the way of wisdom and lead you along
straight paths. When you walk, your steps will
not be hampered; when you run, you will not
stumble.*

We need wisdom to be successful in our recovery. To
have understanding and the ability to make recovery work is worth whatever we may have to sacrifice. To esteem wisdom brings exaltation in our
lives. As we successfully work the steps of recovery, it brings us in touch with people who need our
help. Our wisdom draws people to us. That wisdom
of recovery will add years not only to our own lives
but to the lives of those with whom we share our
recovery. Everyone benefits from our understanding. Recovery cannot be hidden under a basket; it
must be shared. This kind of sharing encourages
those who may be struggling and discouraged.

What a gift of wisdom the Twelve Steps are to
our lives, steps that lead us in a straight way, that
are not hampered, that do not stumble. Indeed this

life-style of wisdom is worth whatever price we pay, and the crown of splendor that we wear is a constant blessing.

O God, teach me your wisdom through the steps of recovery I take.

Proverbs 4: 18–19

The path of the righteous is like the first gleam of dawn, shining ever brighter till the full light of day. But the way of the wicked is like deep darkness; they do not know what makes them stumble.

What a wonderful description of the contrast in our lives before and after recovery, from deep darkness to the first gleam of dawn shining brighter and brighter as we mature in our understanding and wisdom about God and the Twelve Steps. Thinking back to those days of darkness and the stumbling, confused, unsure steps we made causes us to feel even better about our lives now. During the early days of being without our drugs or relationships we felt overwhelming grief and loss. As we continue to work the Steps, our loss begins to turn into gain, and we begin to see the first gleam of dawn.

That was only the beginning of the light we would see. As recovery grows, life grows; as life develops, hope matures and there is something wonderful to look forward to each day. Solomon's wisdom continues to encourage our journey of recovery as we are able to look back and remember where we have come from, to look forward as the journey continues to unfold. Our recovery before and after is like walking out of a storm cloud into the sunshine.

Father, thank you for the contrast in my life that recovery is making possible.

Proverbs 4: 23–27

Above all else, guard your heart, for it is the wellspring of life. Put away perversity from your mouth, keep corrupt talk far from your lips. Let your eyes look straight ahead, fix your gaze directly before you. Make level paths for your feet and take only ways that are firm. Do not swerve to the right or the left; keep your foot from evil.

For recovery to mature, we fix our eyes on the goal of emotional, spiritual, and physical well-being. We continue to look at that regardless of what happens to discourage our plan. We protect our hearts, our intellects, emotions, and wills, because it is from the heart that we live. For the best interest of our recovery we are very choosy about where we walk and very careful about the turns we make. At all costs we protect the work of recovery that God has begun in us. Recovery is so important that we are encouraged to watch what we talk about and to monitor our speech. As we develop relationships with others who struggle against addiction/codependency and are winning the battle, we become more determined to keep making those positive, sure steps.

Each day we walk the walk and talk the talk of recovery, and it becomes second nature to us. Recovery is no longer merely a program we are working but it becomes our very life. Recovery and life have become so enmeshed that we no longer think of them separately.

O God, give me sure, strong goals that mature my recovery.

Proverbs 5: 21–23

For a man's ways are in full view of the Lord,
and he examines all his paths. The evil deeds of a
wicked man ensnare him; the cords of his sin
hold him fast. He will die for lack of discipline,
led astray by his own great folly.

Solomon and his great wisdom plus the Twelve
Steps combine to take us into the deeper levels of
recovery, the adult stages. When we were still active in our addiction/codependency, we were constantly being ensnared by our deeds, and we were
constantly catching ourselves in the web we had
woven through our lack of discipline. How did we
ever think that we could do our own thing and not
pay the consequences?

Through working the Twelve Steps we come to
realize that God knows how to disentangle us, and
if we allow him, he will cut the cords of sin that
hold us in bondage. The Steps teach us the needed
discipline to help us stay free of our greatest folly.
They train us to walk the path of freedom. We learn
that God knows us completely and that he only
wants what is best for us. Therefore we learn to
trust his direction for our recovery.

Life is a maturing process, as is recovery. We
begin on a certain level of understanding and grow
in our understanding as we continue the journey.
We no longer feel compelled to try to run our lives
or the lives of others.

Lord, you have brought me to freedom, and I am
so grateful.

Proverbs 6: 27–28

Can a man scoop fire into his lap without his clothes being burned? Can a man walk on hot coals without his feet being scorched?

In the earlier stages of our recovery, we may have tried to convince ourselves that at some point we would have our disease under enough control that we could toy with our drugs of choice or the unhealthy ways we have of relating. The more mature we become in our recovery, the more we realize that our addiction/codependency is still a potentially dangerous area. As long as we walk the narrow pathway of recovery, we avoid the return to bondage, but if we think we can compromise a little here or there, we'll get burned. The potential for recovery is tremendous, as long as we work our program. The potential for relapse is just as great if we fail to abstain or fail to work the Steps. We can never take fire into our bosom without the consequence of our clothes being burned; likewise, we can never play with our addiction/codependency without the possibility of falling back into the pit. Let us lay aside forever the idea that we may someday be able to control our addiction/codependency.

God, remind me that I can't control my disease of addiction/codependency.

Proverbs 6: 30–31

Men do not despise a thief if he steals to satisfy
his hunger when he is starving. Yet if he is
caught, he must pay sevenfold, though it costs
him all the wealth of his house.

It is difficult to make amends for the things we have
done during our addiction/codependency. How
much easier it would be just to feel bad about it,
confess it to the Lord and our sponsor, and forget
about it. But Solomon reminds us that even a thief
who steals to satisfy his hunger must pay back more
than he took. Another word for amends is restitution. Before recovery, we could slide by with a
sheepish, "I'm sorry," but the Twelve-Steps way of
doing things is different. To take responsibility for
our wrongs is painful, but as we are able to do that,
we become freer. True repentance is more than just
admitting our wrong; it involves paying for what
we have done, even to the extent that we suffer
some personal loss, if need be. This telegraphs the
message that we are sorry and that the other person matters to us. It helps mend the relationship
and restores what has been taken away. Sometimes
we only have to be willing to make amends rather
than actually do it, but when our heart is willing,
the work of restoration is well on its way.

O Father, show me how to make amends to those
I've wronged.

Proverbs 8: 6

Listen, for I have worthy things to say; I open my lips to speak what is right.

The wisdom of recovery is spoken in thousands of meetings. Recovering people speak worthy things as they share their stories of recovery. What we receive from their personal struggles can be exactly what we need to hear to keep us moving along on our own journeys. When we are down, discouraged, lonely, or angry, perhaps ready to give up, it is good to hear someone else tell of similar feelings and how they made it.

Recovery may be very difficult on some days, and on those days we'd probably rather isolate ourselves. But that is precisely when we need to listen to the worthy, encouraging, wise things others have to say. No one ever said that recovery would be easy or that we'd always want to attend the Twelve-Step meetings; but how important it is to avail ourselves of each opportunity we have. Alone in our misery, we will not make it, but together, sharing worthwhile advice and helpful antidotes, we can strengthen each other's recovery.

Father, help me listen to the stories of others and share my own story.

Proverbs 8: 18–21

With me are riches and honor, enduring wealth
and prosperity. My fruit is better than fine gold;
what I yield surpasses choice silver. I walk in the
way of righteousness, along the paths of justice,
bestowing wealth on those who love me and
making their treasuries full.

Wisdom is a rich gift because being wise brings with
it many other wonderful things. When we first
began the journey of recovery, it was like planting a
seed in good soil, but we had no idea what we had
planted. We didn't know that we had invested in a
lifetime of treasure and that the recovery we were
working on would touch more than just our addic-
tion/codependency.

As our recovery progresses, our finances begin to
recover and our self-esteem begins to improve. Our
spirit begins to respond to the healing process of
the Steps, and our ideas of what life means begin to
get better as our attitude improves. Even our ideas
about wealth begin to change. We realize that there
is much more to wealth than money. Indeed, the
steps have brought us to a place of wealth that has
little to do with our bank accounts. Our treasuries
are full now because our lives, health, relationships,
pocketbooks, bodies, souls, and spirits are being restored through the Twelve Steps as we are faithful to
work them.

Father, you certainly have rewarded my search for
treasure by giving me the Twelve Steps.

Proverbs 8: 35–36

*For whoever finds me finds life and receives favor
from the Lord. But whoever fails to find me
harms himself; all who hate me love death.*

Wisdom leads us to life and gives us favor with the
Lord. The wisdom of the Twelve-Step journey to recovery also leads us to life. Our addiction/co-
dependency harmed us and day by day led us
toward death. Each day was a living death as we
existed in its unhappy bondage. Our lives were consumed, our health, our loved ones, our money.
There was no joy or happiness. Yet how difficult it
was to leave that for many of us. As hurtful as it
was, it was a familiar way of life. We were able to
see the destructive outcome as we faced the bottom
of our disease. We began to receive wisdom. We
were able to let go of the drug, alcohol, relationship
and begin steps of recovery.

Each day we obtain more wisdom as we work
the Steps, attend sessions, grow in our concept of
God, allow God to show us our foolish ways of
thinking. This wisdom makes us stronger in our determination to recover at all costs.

What a difference recovery makes. Once we
walked resolutely toward death; now we walk absolutely into life. God, the Twelve Steps and our
willingness to cooperate have brought us to life.

*O God, thank you for the wisdom you have given others
who have walked the road of recovery before me.*

Proverbs 9: 4–6

*"Let all who are simple come in here!" she says
to those who lack judgment. "Come, eat my food
and drink the wine I have mixed. Leave your
simple ways and you will live; walk in the way
of understanding."*

All of life's events can become our schoolteacher if
we let them. Everything we have experienced, both
good and bad, can train us. Wherever we lack wisdom or understanding, we can learn. Before we actively entered recovery, we were unwise in many
areas of living. Being introduced to the Twelve
Steps showed us a healthy way to handle our ad-
diction/codependency. Those same Twelve Steps
cover so much more than just getting clean from
our drugs of choice or free from our codependency.
The wisdom of those simple yet profound Steps can
help heal relationships, can improve every difficult
job problem. Every attitude can be adjusted as we
work those steps. To recover is to walk in the way of
understanding and life. Nothing we have gone
through in our lives is ever wasted. God in his wisdom knows how to use life as our seminary training for whatever his purpose for our lives may be.
As we allow life to teach us and the Twelve Steps
to train us, the outcome will be serenity.

*O God, thank you for the fact that you use life and
the Twelve Steps to train me.*

Proverbs 9: 10–12

The fear of the Lord is the beginning of wisdom,
and knowledge of the Holy One is understanding.
For through me your days will be many, and
years will be added to your life. If you are wise,
your wisdom will reward you; if you are a
mocker, you alone will suffer.

Once more Solomon shows us the contrast of where
we once were and where God is taking us as we
journey toward recovery. Once, in our addic-
tion/codependency, we mocked, put down, and be-
littled those who tried to help us. Those who
reached out to us were pushed aside as we continued on the downward journey. What a sad thing to
remember!

But, thank God, our lives didn't stop there.
Wisdom helped us see that the bottom we hit wasn't
a very pleasant place to be, and we started the upward climb. As we come from an awareness of our
powerlessness over our unmanageable lives, we
begin to understand that only God can reach to
where we find ourselves. As we turn our lives and
wills over to him, he begins to turn our dying into
life and our dead end into beautiful freedom.

Truly the wisdom of recovery rewards us, giving us another chance, a new lease on life. What a
great plan God gave when he showed us the way
to wholeness through recovery.

O God, you have changed me from a mocker into one
who understands.

Proverbs 10: 31–32

The mouth of the righteous brings forth wisdom,
but a perverse tongue will be cut out. The lips
of the righteous know what is fitting, but the
mouth of the wicked only what is perverse.

The words we speak and the thoughts we think create what we feel. We sometimes feel distress in recovery simply because we have talked or thought ourselves into it. "Stinking thinking" is a term familiar to recovering people; but more than a term, it's a real condition that we must constantly fight. It is easy to allow thoughts to control our lives. Those thoughts create emotions, and we have a tendency to respond from those emotions. Our behavior and reactions originate in our thinking. We defile ourselves as we get involved in what-ifs, should-haves, and daydreams of what may happen.

Much of our distress, anger, confusion, discouragement, anxiety, fear, and depression could be alleviated, if not completely eliminated, by watching the meditation of our hearts.

The well part of us, the part active in recovery, is righteous. The unhealed part, the sick part, will speak only negative, perverse words. Let's begin watching the words we meditate on and change course as soon as we detect the destructive ones.

Father, give me courage to face the thoughts that cause
me to stumble and to correct them.

Proverbs 11: 1–3

The Lord abhors dishonest scales, but accurate weights are his delight. When pride comes, then comes disgrace, but with humility comes wisdom. The integrity of the upright guides them, but the unfaithful are destroyed by their duplicity.

Pride will keep us addicted. Pride will never allow us to admit our powerlessness, and of course it will never let us admit our wrongdoings or make amends. Pride will hinder our ability to look at ourselves honestly and take an inventory. Pride is one of the biggest character defects from which we have to recover.

Pride says we are always right. Pride demands its own way. Pride refuses to see anyone else's point of view. Pride causes us to have a rebellious attitude. The end of pride is always disgrace and shame. Maybe a solution to pride would be to list it as one of our weaknesses on our inventory and then to admit our powerlessness over it. As we come to see that pride is a major problem and that we alone cannot change it, we begin to ask the Lord to work on it. Then real change can happen. As we confess our wrongs to someone, our pride is broken, and, according to the proverb, humility brings wisdom. What a contrast and what a wonderfully positive step in our recovery!

Father, I bring you the pride I see within myself and I ask you to show me any hidden pride.

Proverbs 11: 4

Wealth is worthless in the day of wrath, but righteousness delivers from death.

Righteousness is not something we do in our own strength. Righteousness doesn't happen because we abstain from our drug of choice or codependent behavior. Righteousness isn't even the result of our not hurting someone else. Righteousness is the work that only God can produce within our inner person as we give our lives and wills over to him. Self-righteousness is what we have accomplished by sheer determination and by our own natural ability. But self-righteousness doesn't constitute a real change or a permanent one. It is easy to be proud about our great successes in recovery if we are self-righteous. True righteousness is the result of knowing our own worthlessness, our own weakness, and our own failure and yet knowing God's willingness to take us on and change us from the inside out. That's it! Self-righteousness is our trying to change from the outside in. True righteousness is God's changing us from the inside out. We are dependent on God for the real and permanent change.

O God, help me lay aside my righteousness and accept your true righteousness.

Proverbs 11: 5–6

*The righteousness of the blameless makes a
straight way for them, but the wicked are brought
down by their own wickedness. The
righteousness of the upright delivers them, but
the unfaithful are trapped by evil desires.*

If we are to recover, we have to get to the place
where we can accept the fact that we chose our life
of addiction/codependency. We didn't fall into it by
accident. Rather, our own character defects led us
into this dependency. Addiction/codependency
was not our goal; no one plans to become an ad-
dict/codependent. We just wanted to ease the pain,
fill the lonely hours, feel better about ourselves, and
we started using something or someone. For a while
it may have seemed to be working, but soon enough
we were trapped. Our addiction/codependency
consumed more and more of our lives and gave less
and less satisfaction, and we had no control over
our will. Nothing we did made any difference.
Promises not to do it again were broken as we'd
struggle, only to fall back into the old ways. Time
and time again we'd fail to do what we knew was
the right thing until at last we knew that we were
hopelessly trapped.

   Until we came to this place there was no hope
for recovery, but in our helpless and powerless condition we could turn to God and allow him to transform us.

*O God, reach into the traps I set for myself and free me
to walk in your ways.*

Proverbs 11: 7

When a wicked man dies, his hope perishes; all he expected from his power comes to nothing.

Something in each of us feels the need to be in control—of our lives, plans, relationships, feelings, and destiny. Somehow we believe that we have the power to control. We even try to exert control over the lives of those around us.

Since the beginning of time the issue has always been humanity's idea that our way is better than God's way, that we know better how to run our lives. The question to us has always been, Will you submit your will to the will of God? We don't realize that we are in rebellion when we try to run our lives and that rebellion will lead us to destruction. All our great plans have actually come to nothing. All we expected our power to accomplish is nothing. In recovery we have to be reminded constantly of our powerlessness. We have power only to admit that we are powerless. What an uncomfortable place to be. How vulnerable.

Father, help me to lay down what I perceive to be my power and allow you to be my power.

Proverbs 11: 8

The righteous man is rescued from trouble, and it comes on the wicked instead.

In our journey of recovery, let's think of the "righteous man" as the recovering person. In that light, as we recover, we are rescued from trouble. Our recovery takes us step by step out of the trouble we once created by our addiction/codependency. As we learn new ways of handling life's problems and new coping skills, trouble is no longer so overwhelming and consuming. As we develop new behaviors and appropriate responses to life, we create less and less trouble for ourselves.

God doesn't usually just zap us out of trouble like many of us wish he would. Rather he leads us through whatever mess we are in and trains us as he leads us out. Anytime we decide that recovery is not for us and we fall back into the ways of our wicked addiction/codependency, trouble will once more overtake us and consume our lives. Each of us decides by our daily actions whether we will walk in recovery and be free of the trouble addiction produced or be controlled by the storms of devastation that we once walked in regularly. Today we can be rescued from the old life-style and the trouble it represents.

O God, help me to choose to allow you to rescue me from trouble as I recover.

Proverbs 11: 9–11

With his mouth the godless destroys his neighbor,
but through knowledge the righteous escape.
When the righteous prosper, the city rejoices;
when the wicked perish, there are shouts of joy.
Through the blessing of the upright a city is
exalted, but by the mouth of the wicked it is
destroyed.

We can destroy a person with our mouths. Even
though what we say may need to be said, it is so
easy to cut a person to shreds by our tone and our
words. Often in the midst of our addiction/code-
pendency and even in the early stages of recovery
when we are in so much pain, we can thoughtlessly
say things that wound to the core. Sometimes in trying to prove our point, we can leave the other person devastated. Some of us need to register our
tongue with the authorities as a deadly weapon.

As we mature in our recovery, we begin to learn
how to guard our words and temper them so they
are not so painful. Words are either a curse or a
blessing, and we determine which comes from our
mouths. Knowledge teaches us how to verbalize
negative emotions without devastating the other
person. Knowledge trains us to confront a situation
and yet leave the other person's worth as a person
still intact.

Lord, teach me to speak from my heart only those words
that encourage another's recovery.

Proverbs 11: 12–13

*A man who lacks judgment derides his neighbor,
but a man of understanding holds his tongue. A
gossip betrays a confidence, but a trustworthy
man keeps a secret.*

In the journey of recovery, speech plays an important part. What we say to ourselves is of paramount importance. But just as important is what we say about others and to others. Often we verbalize things that are better left unsaid, while leaving important words unspoken.

In recovery it is important for us who are working the Fifth Step to know that our inventory is safe with the person with whom we share it. We would be quite embarrassed if others knew the secrets we are so ashamed of. Just as crucial is our ability to keep someone else's secrets safe. In our meetings we walk in the very depths of people's hearts as we hear their stories. In closed meetings we dig through the ugly and often unacceptable human feelings we experience as we struggle through difficult days of recovery. Just as we do not want anyone to share our deepest feelings with others, we need to guard the hearts of those we hear. Rather than expose those around us, let's cover them and protect them. It's easy to be critical of those who are not where we are, but instead let's extend understanding.

*Father, help me to guard my tongue and to protect
the secrets of others.*

Proverbs 11: 14

For lack of guidance a nation falls, but many advisers make victory sure.

Many of us had a tendency to isolate ourselves, and we became loners during our days of addiction/co-dependency. Our playmates and the few people close to us were also active in their addiction/code-pendency. We had a tendency to avoid those who were critical of our addiction/codependency, and we didn't invite much advice from them. By contrast, as recovering people, we need the advice, correction, encouragement, and wisdom of others in recovery.

We are taught to reach out to someone else when we are fighting the urge to use. Our inventory means that we become open to a fellow traveler. Our sponsor is to be a source of wise counsel and, of course, the meetings we attend give us guidance and direction and hope as others share their stories. Isolation kept us bound, kept us defeated and ad-dicted/codependent. Communion with others keeps us going in the right direction. Isolation keeps us bound to our old mindsets and attitudes. Becoming open and listening to the advice and wis-dom of those who are successful assure us of con-tinuing freedom. Recovery requires others' involvement, and yet many of us have to force our-selves to let anyone close.

Father, give me courage to accept others' advice and counsel who are successful in recovery.

Proverbs 11: 15

He who puts up security for another will surely suffer, but whoever refuses to strike hands in pledge is safe.

Many who are in recovery are also codependents. We feel called to make the world better. We take care of others, enable and rescue and do it all in the name of love. Our project is anyone who is in a mess, anyone who is needy, or anyone who is unhealthy. Somehow we feel responsible for everyone else's pain and unhappiness, and we do everything possible to heal them. We make promises we cannot keep and wear ourselves out trying to be superperson in others' lives. We pledge our very lives, our very being in our endeavor to fix this hurting person. We insist on always being there for them and having unconditional love for them. Our life focus turns from God, self-care, and others to *the* other, neglecting and abandoning ourselves and God. Our lives become greatly out of balance as we become more and more enmeshed in this person's life.

The overwhelming fact is that no human love, regardless how great, is sufficient to heal anyone else. So we must learn to do only what God anoints us to do in that person's life and that is to love God and take care of ourselves. Then we are in the safety of recovery.

O God, give me wisdom to know that I am not called to heal anyone else.

Proverbs 11: 16–17

A kindhearted woman gains respect, but ruthless
men gain only wealth. A kind man benefits
himself, but a cruel man brings himself harm.

One of the deeper changes that God wants to make
in our recovery is in our hardness of heart. As ad-
dicts/codependents, we sometimes develop the defense mechanism of a hard, harsh, ruthless attitude.
This prevents many well-meaning people from
touching the real person inside us. Their words of
exhortation about our addiction/codependency are
stopped by our thick walls of protection. As we
walk deeper into the journey of recovery, God begins to soften those tough areas, tenderizing and
restoring the ability to be kindhearted. As he
changes our hearts and attitudes, we allow ourselves to become vulnerable, and we are more willing to be open. Our porcupine needles of protection
fade away, and we allow people to see the real us.

This part of recovery may be discovered in our
Fourth Step, but it may be a while before we are able
to allow the Lord to transform and remove those
defects from us. This one change is a major difference between living a sober life-style and abstaining
from our drugs of choice.

O God, change me from ruthless and cruel into a
kind and caring person.

Proverbs 11: 18–19

The wicked man earns deceptive wages, but he
who sows righteousness reaps a sure reward.
The truly righteous man attains life, but he who
pursues evil goes to his death.

In our journey of recovery in conjunction with the
Proverbs, let's think of the evil or wicked man as
that person we were before recovery, along with
that part of us that is still unrecovered. This helps us
see why we need to work the Twelve Steps for the
rest of our lives. The righteous person is the healthy,
recovering part of us. There is always a battle between the two of us, always a struggle. When we
give in to the unhealed part of ourselves, there will
be a payday. When we allow our recovering part to
be in charge, there will be a reward. We've been in
recovery long enough to know that our addic-
tion/codependency will lead us down the path of
destruction and death. The way of recovery is the
way of life. Our Father restores us to sane living
through the process of recovery. God is willing. The
Twelve Steps are available. The goals of both pathways are clearly outlined for us in Scripture. The
choice is ours. Which wage will we choose?

O God, help me daily choose the pathway of recovery
and life.

Proverbs 11: 20–21

*The Lord detests men of perverse heart but he
delights in those whose ways are blameless. Be
sure of this: The wicked will not go unpunished,
but those who are righteous will go free.*

In recovery we are looking at the difference between
bondage and freedom. Two different life-styles, two
different destinations, two different journeys. One
journey seems easier, the pain is quietly numbed.
We are not responsible. Someone else takes care of
us, protects us, picks up after us, rescues us; but
after all we are hopelessly in bondage. The end will
be death, if not physical death, at least death to our
self-respect, health, spirituality, emotions, and significant relationships. That is the cost of bondage,
quite a price for a way that seemed easier.

On the other hand is the journey that gives us
freedom. There is a price for that adventure also.
Our pain is not numbed. Rather we are forced to
face and feel each pain. We do have some support
people through our Twelve-Step programs, but they
confront us with more responsibility than we care to
take. No one excuses or rescues us, but they are always there if we mean business. Quite a price, but
the outcome of that journey is freedom.

*O God, help me evaluate the cost of the journey
by the destination.*

Proverbs 11: 22–23

*Like a gold ring in a pig's snout is a beautiful
woman who shows no discretion. The desire of
the righteous ends only in good, but the hope of
the wicked only in wrath.*

So often as a child I was told "pretty is as pretty
does."

As men and women in recovery, our counte-
nance often discloses what is really going on inside.
Lack of peace is easily seen on our faces. Anger, as
well as joy, is manifested on our faces. Yet beauty of
face never covers up for lack of discretion. Our actions and our speech can undo and discredit our
outward looks in just a few seconds. To be careful
about what we say and do is very important in recovery. To be prudent in the way we deal with people, to be sensitive to their pain and frustration
rather than responding to them from impulse or
anger, to learn to love the principles we have
learned in our Twelve Steps, and to practice them
in all our affairs are certainly the purposes and goals
of recovery.

Many abstain from their drug of choice, but because they want only to be clean, dry, or drug-free,
they miss the deeper meaning of recovery, a change
so real and so deep that we are never the same
again. The Twelve Steps can be life changing, making us much more than pretty faces, instead making us beautiful people.

*O God, please change more than just my substance use.
Change me.*

Proverbs 11: 24–26

One man gives freely, yet gains even more;
another withholds unduly, but comes to poverty.
A generous man will prosper; he who refreshes
others will himself be refreshed. People curse the
man who hoards grain, but blessing crowns him
who is willing to sell.

In our pre-recovery days, it was common to withhold blessings and goodness from everyone. In our
disease we were selfish and self-centered and our
addiction/codependency was owner and posses-
sor of body and soul. The disease and its effects
were the center of our lives. Our needs, wants, and
wishes came first. Personal gratification was of
prime importance.

As we begin to recover and live a truly sober life-
style, our focus is still on ourselves but in a more
healthy way; now it has become self-care, a proper
love for ourselves. As our focus changes, we are
able to reach out of ourselves to others. As we bless
those around us, we find that we also begin to reap
those benefits. The law of sowing and reaping also
involves increase. We notice that we gain as we
give.

As we grow in our recovery we also find that we
can carry the message of recovery to others, and
every time we share our story or the Twelve Steps,
we ourselves will be refreshed. As we give away
the wonderful news of hope, our own recovery is
strengthened. Recovery can lead us away from the

selfish and self-centered into a balanced self-care and concern for others that promotes healing.

Father, thank you for looking beyond my selfish ways and seeing the potential for self-care and a healthy care for others.

Proverbs 11: 29–31

He who brings trouble on his family will inherit only wind, and the fool will be servant to the wise. The fruit of the righteous is a tree of life, and he who wins souls is wise. If the righteous receive their due on earth, how much more the ungodly and the sinner!

Before recovery each of us brought trouble to those around us. Our families suffered greatly because of our addiction/codependency. Many times we look back with sorrow at the hurts we inflicted on those we love, and yet our being sorry does not undo what we have done. We may have been reaping the wind in the way our spouses, parents, children, or friends reacted to us.

But, praise the Lord, that was before recovery. Through recovery God is not only changing our addiction/codependency but reconciling us to himself, and he is working to bring reconciliation to those relationships we have damaged. We slowly begin to change, and others see and feel the change. Sometimes they begin to trust us again. Making amends for what we have done also helps to bridge the gap and restore confidence. As we continue to grow in our recovery, we may struggle with our continuing personal inventories, especially when we are wrong. But it is this Step of promptly admitting our wrongs that at last convinces others of the real change recovery is bringing about in our lives.

Then we become the fruit of righteousness as our lives reflect the power of recovery to our families and to those not yet in recovery.

O God, thank you for the hope that my family can be restored as I recover.

Proverbs 12: 1

Whoever loves discipline loves knowledge, but he
who hates correction is stupid.

Solomon certainly doesn't mince words. The before
and after recovery picture is described very well in
this proverb. Before recovery we not only hated correction but also refused to take any responsibility
for anything in our lives. We insisted we weren't
even to blame for our addiction/codependency.
Looking back, it's easy to see the stupidity of ad-
dictive/codependent thinking.

Many of us had to be taught and trained in the
ways and means of addiction/codependency in
those early stages of recovery. We listened to others' stories. We may have gone into a treatment center, a Twelve-Step program, or an outpatient
program. Education is one of the keys to unlocking
the doors of addiction/codependency. With knowledge about the addiction/codependency comes the
wisdom to discipline ourselves and to change the
old addictive/codependent life-style. No longer
stupid, we begin to appreciate and accept the correction of others in recovery, others who have our
best interest at heart. Recovery is knowledge and
discipline and the result is freedom.

O God, teach me to accept correction and to love
discipline and knowledge.

Proverbs 12: 2–3

A good man obtains favor from the Lord, but the Lord condemns a crafty man. A man cannot be established through wickedness, but the righteous cannot be uprooted.

Oh, what crafty persons we were during our days of addiction/codependency. We could convince almost anyone about anything. During this time, even though the Lord was merciful, his blessing could not be on us. Our old ways condemned us. How different we become as we continue to walk the pathway of recovery. We came to realize that we could never be established through the wickedness our addiction/codependency encouraged. Our recovery leads us into favor with God. We begin to really understand his love for us, even when it is demonstrated through discipline. As long as we continue to walk faithfully in the ways of recovery and Twelve Steps, we cannot be uprooted. Recovery cements us into life in such a way that the storms of life cannot uproot us, the offenses of people cannot uproot us, problems with jobs or finances cannot cause us to fall. We may bend like trees during a windstorm, but our roots only go deeper and we become more secure, steadier, surer in our daily lives. Recovery really does work.

O God, thank you for changing me from being a crafty person to being a person who cannot be uprooted.

Proverbs 12: 11

He who works his land will have abundant food,
but he who chases fantasies lacks judgment.

Until we began working the Twelve Steps to recovery, we each had some kind of fantasy, some sort of illusion, some deception that kept us in bondage to our drug of choice. It was much easier to believe the lie than it was to face the fact that we were hopelessly addicted/codependent. Our lack of judgment is demonstrated by the length of time we remained addicted/codependent.

As we begin and continue the journey into recovery, we find that the Twelve Steps won't work unless we do. Recovery doesn't happen unless, like the farmer who works his land, we work our plan. Our faithfulness to our recovery assures that we will experience abundant life. If the farmer does his part and mother nature cooperates, there should be an abundance of food. In recovery we don't have to depend on the weather. We work the program, and God is faithful to do his part. Recovery is sure! Abundant recovery. From time to time we may remember the fantasy, the illusion that we chased during the past, but we are no longer held in captivity. We see it for what it is, and we go on and continue to take faithful and consistent steps.

O God, make me mindful of the fantasies that would
prevent me from working my plan.

Proverbs 12: 15–17

*The way of a fool seems right to him, but a
wise man listens to advice. A fool shows his
annoyance at once, but a prudent man overlooks
an insult. A truthful witness gives honest
testimony, but a false witness tells lies.*

Look how long we were foolish, thinking that our
life-style of addiction/codependency was the answer to our pain and problems. Our way seemed
right, it felt right to us, but our way only robbed us
of real life. Because we were unwise, we wouldn't
listen to anyone when confronted about our addic-
tion/codependency, and we stayed bound.

If we are in recovery, we are wise! If we are wise,
we listen to advice, we weigh others' opinions, we
gather information to apply to the situations we
face. God, together with our recovery plan, is
changing us from being fools into being wise and
productive people.

It's easier to show our irritation toward people
when we are not in an active program of recovery.
We fly off the handle, snap at people, responding
from our own anger and irritation. As we grow in
recovery, we become able to overlook the insults
and ugly attitudes of others without stuffing the
negative emotions. We can look at the negative
emotions and process them in an appropriate way.
As we learn to value ourselves and others, we are

able to learn new ways of coping with irritation, leaving everyone's sense of dignity intact.

O God, help me to submit willingly to the right way
as I relinquish what I have perceived to be
the right way.

Proverbs 12: 18

Reckless words pierce like a sword, but the tongue of the wise brings healing.

In our time of addiction/codependency, reckless words may have often poured forth from us. Anyone in the path of our words was sure to be angered, wounded, pierced to the core.

As we begin to recover, we become aware of our responsibility for our words. We can train ourselves to be more gentle, more cautious about our verbal responses. The early steps of recovery help us to become aware and to do what we can to change the old addictive/codependent ways of handling conflict and speaking to people. But as we continue to recover and mature in our recovery, our words can actually bring hope, help, and healing to those we have wounded. As we do our Fourth and Fifth Steps, and then begin to make amends, we will be a source of healing. As those we have hurt begin to see and hear the change within us, our words begin to be a healing balm on their hearts. Words have tremendous power, and when we are recovering ourselves, we will be a source of healing words.

Our words can also transmit hope to those who are still struggling, who are discouraged, who are just beginning the journey.

O God, give me words that heal those who hurt.

Proverbs 12: 25

An anxious heart weighs a man down, but a kind word cheers him up.

Addicts/codependents haven't cornered the market on anxious hearts, but we are certainly well aware of the heaviness of spirit that anxious thoughts can bring. In our stressful world, everyone knows the strain of finances, concerns over health, family problems. We can all relate to the anxiety our fast culture encourages.

Within our own hearts, with our personal meditation, we can lift or crush our hearts. Whatever we allow ourselves to meditate on will have an effect in our emotions. As we learn to guard the words we say to ourselves, about ourselves, about life, about our recovery and our relationships, we can control the negative emotions we feel. Learning to speak kind, hopeful, encouraging words to ourselves can actually cheer us. It's nice to have others speak kindly to us, but why wait for someone else? We can begin speaking those words that bring cheer regardless of what others do. The words of our mouth or the meditation of our hearts originates in exactly the same place, our mind, and we do have the ability to change those patterns.

O God, teach me to encourage myself.

Proverbs 12: 26

A righteous man is cautious in friendship, but the way of the wicked leads them astray.

It's easy to see that before we began our Twelve-Step recovery, our way continually led us astray. We had trouble making and holding onto friendships with nonaddicted people. They had nothing in common with us, they tried to talk us into abstaining from our drug of choice, they meddled with our lives. We just didn't want to be bothered with people who "didn't understand" us. After getting clean, we may have continued some of those friendships for a while, but we didn't mix as well as we once did. For a while we may have even fought the advice of other recovering people to make new friends. But as we build up some "clean time," we begin to be more cautious about our friends, choosing those who are traveling the same pathway. It's much more comfortable to talk with those who are familiar with the struggle on hard days and can just stand by and give support. The friends we choose often reflect where we are in our recovery. If we are still comfortable with those who are not recovering, we may need to re-evaluate. Those we want to spend quality time with reflect the true degree of recovery we experience.

Father, help me to choose friends that will facilitate my recovery.

Proverbs 13: 2–3

From the fruit of his lips a man enjoys good things, but the unfaithful have a craving for violence. He who guards his lips guards his life, but he who speaks rashly will come to ruin.

Solomon has a great deal to say about the mouth and words and the effect they have in our lives. Especially in recovery, words are very important. When we speak positive, hopeful, encouraging words, we are speaking wisdom from the recovering, healing part of ourselves. From that part of our being we bring forth good fruit, and we enjoy the results. When we are discouraged or having a bad day, when we feel sorry for ourselves or are experiencing anger, it is easy to speak impulsively. Words are powerful and have the ability to take us from an OK day to the pits of despair in just minutes. Our words can ruin the entire day. Therefore it is wisdom, it is recovery, to guard our lips, to monitor the words we speak. Our recovery today depends on the words we say, to ourselves as well as to others. To control the tongue may be one of the most difficult tasks in our recovery, but it will be one of the most beneficial things we do.

Lord, set a watch at my mouth and help me guard what I say today.

Proverbs 13: 9–10

The light of the righteous shines brightly, but the lamp of the wicked is snuffed out. Pride only breeds quarrels, but wisdom is found in those who take advice.

Our life of addiction/codependency was actually mere existence. No light came from us because we were terminally ill with the disease of addiction/codependency. Our entire life was snuffed out by the controlling substance/relationship. Oh, what a difference recovery makes. Our lives are being restored, and the light of health shines from within. Our once-dim eyes now have a sparkle, our once-staggering steps now are stable, with a spring to them. Even our skin tone has brightened as we have experienced the health that recovery gives. The results of recovery that those around us see in our lives are testimonies for those who still struggle with their addiction/codependency. Those who know where we once were and have watched us fight the disease know the power those simple, spiritual Twelve Steps can have in an addict/codependent's life.

Our recovery can also be seen in something as simple as our willingness to accept advice, especially when it isn't what we want to hear. Once we were so quick to know exactly what we wanted to do, but recovery has increased our willingness to wait, to listen, and to evaluate. Recovery is wisdom!

O God, thank you for the brightness I can see because of the changes recovery has produced.

Proverbs 13: 12–14

*Hope deferred makes the heart sick, but a long-
ing fulfilled is a tree of life. He who scorns
instruction will pay for it, but he who respects
a command is rewarded. The teaching of the
wise is a fountain of life, turning a man from the
snares of death.*

Addiction and codependency are truly ways of
death. It is difficult to admit that something we had
given ourselves over to for so long was actually a
snare of death, but it is true. We mourn the many
days we wasted, but we are quick to remind ourselves that we now are making each day count.
Some wise teacher found the words that at last
began to rescue us from the way that was leading
to death. As we listened to the instruction of someone who had been there too, we knew there was
hope. How drastically our lives have changed
through the simple yet profound plan of recovery.

The Twelve Steps teach us to share the good
news with others who are struggling. As we continue to tell our story, we become fountains of life
to others. Everyone may not be ready when we first
share our stories, but the seeds have been planted.
When they hit the bottom, the plan of recovery will
begin to grow with them. This fountain of life that
we commonly refer to as the Twelve Steps will continue to touch the lives of those in the snare of death
and will offer new life.

*Father, thank you for the fountain of life that rescued
me from death.*

Proverbs 13: 17

A wicked messenger falls into trouble, but a
trustworthy envoy brings healing.

Before we entered our Twelve-Step plan of recovery,
we could hardly be trusted. Our addiction/code-
pendency controlled so much of our lives that we
had little emotional energy left for being depend-
able. We meant well, our intentions were good, but
somehow we got distracted and our good intentions
fell by the wayside. Our addiction/codependency
was definitely a wicked messenger that helped us
fall into trouble often. Many people were disappointed or hurt by our lack of trustworthiness.

As we begin the metamorphosis that true recovery is sure to bring, we may see that not being trustworthy is one of our character flaws. We begin
allowing God to remove that defect of character,
and he trains us to be trustworthy. It takes a while
for those around us to be able to trust us once more,
but little by little trust is restored and healing takes
place in the lives of those we have wounded. When
we are truly in recovery, every area, every relationship is affected. Recovery brings trustworthiness,
which in turn promotes healing.

Father, teach me how to regain the trust I've lost
from other people.

Proverbs 14: 1–2

The wise woman builds her house, but with her own hands the foolish one tears hers down. He whose walk is upright fears the Lord, but he whose ways are devious despises him.

As women in recovery we can think back to those days when our addiction/codependency had our lives so wrapped up that our homes were slowly being torn down, bit by bit. Our attention, our focus in life, was so out of alignment that we didn't even see the signs of neglect. To look back could bring pain even now, if we were not actively pursuing recovery. Wisdom and recovery go together, and as we work our Twelve Steps, we learn more about the ways the disease can rob us. The longer we recover, the more we can build or rebuild those areas of home life that we have allowed to slide. As we desire to see restoration and work toward that goal, we will be rewarded. As we continue to build up what once was torn down, everyone will benefit. There is hope for happiness, wholeness, and unity within our household as we continue to pursue emotional wholeness.

O God, help me rebuild whatever I may have torn down.

Proverbs 14: 3–4

*A fool's talk brings a rod to his back, but the lips
of the wise protect them. Where there are no oxen,
the manger is empty, but from the strength of an
ox comes an abundant harvest.*

"From the abundance of the heart the mouth
speaks" is another Scripture verse that reminds us
that the "real" person is exposed by his or her
words. Wisdom in recovery teaches us that we don't
have to say everything we think or even everything
we think others need to hear. Wisdom is teaching
us to listen more than we speak and then to weigh
what we do speak. We would often draw people's
disapproval or rebukes before recovery because our
speech was unguarded. As addicts/codependents
we could rationalize, excuse, or blame in short
order. It wasn't unusual for our codependent speech
to include sermons and lectures about the dependent person's ways.

As we recover, we realize that our talking hasn't
helped, healed, or fixed the other person; instead it
has helped build higher walls. Much of our recovery is based on working on our individual issues,
and as the contents of our hearts gradually begin to
change, the change is reflected in our speech. Rather
than being a weapon, our speech can become an in-
strument of healing, health, wholeness, and hope.
What a blessing recovery is in every area of life.

*O God, help me to correct the contents of my heart so
that my speech is helpful rather than hurtful.*

Proverbs 14: 7–8

Stay away from a foolish man, for you will not find knowledge on his lips. The wisdom of the prudent is to give thought to their ways, but the folly of fools is deception.

Denial and avoidance in our days of addiction/co-dependency prevented us from being aware of the deception we lived under. At first the stinging awareness was almost too much for us, but as we saw and admitted how foolish, how deceptive we had been, healing began to happen.

Healing through the Twelve Steps encourages us to turn and face what we have avoided. Truth is often painful, and yet we need to experience healing pain. To take the risk of a fearless, searching moral inventory begins the healing process. Failure isn't the end unless we fail to try again. To see the failure is painful, but to turn the failure into a back entrance to success is part of recovery. God is changing, healing, maturing us, and as that happens we become the person who is indeed prudent, who knows how to make life work, how to make the best of negative situations, how to grow through the continuing inventory. Recovery is being able to look back without the stinging pain and rejoice over the distance our recovery has brought us.

O God, guide me as I give thought to my ways.

Proverbs 14: 9–10

Fools mock at making amends for sin, but goodwill is found among the upright. Each heart knows its own bitterness, and no one else can share its joy.

Solomon speaks often of making amends for our sins. The earliest Steps of recovery focus on our addiction/codependency and our powerlessness over it. As we turn our lives and wills over to God and venture into the inventory, we are growing. Maturity in our recovery causes us to look outward to those we have wronged; and when we are truly living our recovery, it is time to make amends. In our immaturity in recovery, we may consider this a bit extreme, but soon enough we will see that making amends is an important Step.

Each one of us has an innermost private person that cannot be shared with anyone. Regardless of how much we desire to have someone touch that part of us, there are things in life that we will face alone. For addicts/codependents that may seem frightening because many of us are already dealing with abandonment issues. Our deep heart, that deepest part of us, cannot be expressed in words to anyone. Only God truly knows and understands that part of us. Only God can face those times of bitter loss and fear with us. Only God can promise to never leave or forsake us and actually keep the promise. Some pains and some joys will be experienced only with our Father.

Father, teach me how to make amends and how to allow you to share in the bitterness and joy that I can't share with anyone else.

Proverbs 14: 13

*Even in laughter the heart may ache, and joy may
end in grief.*

As addicts/codependents we have become masters
at disguise, much like the clown who was in deep
grief but continued his act and made others laugh.
Because of our dysfunctional family of origin, we
may have learned how to get everyone to laugh in
order to change the focus from the crisis. Many of us
smile and look pleasant on the outside, but in reality
our hearts are breaking. We have found a way tem-
porarily to ease, stop, or avoid the pain, and so we
become clowns. It may seem frightening to lay aside
the clown face, to exchange our laughter and jok-
ing for pain, tears, and grief. That is part of recovery—a hard part, yes, but we must face whatever
we have been running away from if we are to mature in recovery. Part of the problem is that what we
have avoided is still part of our lives, and until we
deal with the phantom it will always jump out and
frighten us at the most inopportune times.

*Father, give me courage to stop laughing when I need
to face my tears and pain.*

Proverbs 14: 15–16

A simple man believes anything, but a prudent man gives thought to his steps. A wise man fears the Lord and shuns evil, but a fool is hotheaded and reckless.

What a wonderful difference recovery is making in our lives. Where we once were hotheaded, reckless, inconsistent and gullible, we find that the Twelve Steps are bringing balance, hope, common sense, and wisdom. We are becoming levelheaded. Recovery from addiction/codependency doesn't affect merely our drug of choice; it can change our entire life-style if we allow it. The Steps teach us how to be prudent when before we were flighty. The Steps can bring us to balance in relationships, spiritual life, attitudes, finances, and understanding. Those trusty Steps combined with God's direction through the Word assure us of daily victory—even on days when circumstances and situations come against us to knock us down. Each day as we hold tightly to our program, make the Steps, we become more proficient in recovery. Our once impulsive and compulsive behaviors respond to the course of recovery that our support groups and sponsors help us plan. Indeed, health is the result, and it shows in every area of our lives.

O God, thank you for the changes you have brought about through the Twelve Steps and your Word.

Proverbs 14: 26–27

He who fears the Lord has a secure fortress, and for his children it will be a refuge. The fear of the Lord is a fountain of life, turning a man from the snares of death.

God is a secure fortress for those who are working on recovery. Even on days when emotional storms threaten, there is that place of safety. During the early stages of recovery, the old habit patterns were still firmly in place, and it may have been difficult to run into the safety of the secure fortress. Instead, the old ways of worrying, fretting, inappropriate responses, stinking thinking, and what-ifs crowded in. As we have developed and matured in recovery, we have become better able to stop the old habits and do something profitable. It is such a blessing to realize that as our recovery continues our faith in God grows and that our children's lives will also be affected in a positive way. Just as the addiction/co-dependency is passed to the younger generations, likewise the healing benefits of recovery will be too.

On days when the mountain looks steep and our strength feels weak, God is the place to which we can run, knowing that he is the author of recovery and recovery is written on every page of his Word.

O Lord, thank you for providing a safe and secure place to recover.

Proverbs 14: 28–29

A large population is a king's glory, but without subjects a prince is ruined. A patient man has great understanding, but a quick-tempered man displays folly.

In recovery patience is of paramount importance. Recovery is a day-by-day, sometimes hour-by-hour journey, and no stopwatch is involved, except within ourselves. Our own urgency sometimes puts us in a state of panic and rush. But recovery isn't something we hurry to get through. Recovery is now our way of living, and as we mature in our recovery, we come to understand that we may as well sit back and enjoy the trip. When we are not patient, we constantly put ourselves under stress, and stress can cause us to be short-tempered and to act foolishly. Patience is oftentimes a fruit of maturity. We mellow out and realize that the present situation is only temporary. It will pass. Something new comes along soon, and as the new circumstance teaches us to cope with that situation, patience is being developed. Getting ill about the situation doesn't help; rather it complicates, because now we have not only the trying situation but our unpleasant emotions to deal with. Recovery teaches us that keeping it simple, one day at a time, is the easiest route.

Father, give me the ability to be patient with recovery and with myself.

Proverbs 14: 30–31

*A heart at peace gives life to the body, but envy
rots the bones.*

Once more the proverbs give us a secret that proves
vital in our recovery. Being at peace within ourselves is an absolute must, and as we maintain
peace, our bodies receive strength and life. Before
recovery and possibly in the early stages of recovery, we certainly were not experiencing peace—our
lives were anything but peaceful. Even in the early
stages of recovery, our bodies were in turmoil, our
emotions were topsy-turvy, and there was little
promise of ever experiencing serenity again.

But recovery just normally leads us to peace. As
healing takes place and we are able to turn our lives
and wills over to God, as we surrender our agen-
das and allow God to be in charge, serenity comes.
Our bodies begin to respond to the absence of stress.
Before recovery we were consumed with death. Our
destination was death. It is God's desire to bring
our hearts to peace. He knows that if we can get to
that place, abundant life will be ours. God's purpose in recovery is not just that we abstain from our
drug of choice or the soothing relationship, but that
our life be crowned with serenity.

O God, thank you for serenity and peace of heart.

Proverbs 15: 1–2

A gentle answer turns away wrath, but a harsh word stirs up anger. The tongue of the wise commends knowledge, but the mouth of the fool gushes folly.

Recovery touches every area of our lives. It isn't just abstinence from our addiction/codependency. It improves every area of living. In the past we may have easily responded to those around us with harsh words. No wonder relationships suffered.

As recovery progresses, we learn to weigh what we say, and the wisdom of recovery teaches us to respond with a gentle answer, even when nerves are on edge. Relationships improve with our ability to listen to those around us. The need to be defensive lessens, and growth takes place. Relationships always suffer when we aren't practicing the principles of recovery. Learning to respond with a gentle answer or soft word may take some doing, but it is well worth the effort. The wisdom of recovery teaches us how to control the tongue where before our unwise, unrecovering mouth just gushed forth foolishness and injury.

Lord, thank you for helping my mouth to recover.

Proverbs 15: 4

The tongue that brings healing is a tree of life,
but a deceitful tongue crushes the spirit.

Solomon had much to say about our words,
tongues, and mouths. In recovery we are learning
the importance of our words and the value of si-
lence. Because our entire life was built on deceit and
denial before recovery, our tongues spoke forth
what was already in our hearts. Our hurtful words
crushed the spirits not only of others but ourselves.
Look at the difference recovery is making in the
words we speak and in the tone in which we speak.
Not only that, but as we share our stories of recovery with others our tongues bring healing to them.
It's amazing to think that something as negative as
our addiction/codependency could ever be used to
help. God and our recovery can take the worst
things we have done and change them into something positive. To learn to bridle our tongues shows
that we are maturing in the process of recovery.
Learning to share those things that can encourage,
inspire, help, and correct others causes our tongues
to bring healing and recovery to others.

O God, thank you for turning my tongue into a
blessing through recovery.

Proverbs 15: 8–10

The Lord detests the sacrifice of the wicked, but the prayer of the upright pleases him. The Lord detests the way of the wicked but he loves those who pursue righteousness. Stern discipline awaits him who leaves the path; he who hates correction will die.

Even before we began our Twelve-Step living, God didn't hate us, he detested the ways of addiction/codependency that were stealing our lives, relationships, and health. He hated the way we were choosing to walk because it only would take us to destruction. God is pleased when any of his erring children begin the journey toward wholeness. The steps that brought us to recovery were painful. As we continue the journey, we will occasionally have a tendency to relapse, to leave the path. The consequences can be serious. But even then it is our Father's severe mercy. Our Father wants us to enjoy peace, joy, love, a sound mind, and he knows that our addiction/codependency will rob us of that. In love he corrects our course, not because he is mad, but because he knows how easy it is to get off on the wrong road.

If we accept his correction, we will be back on the road of recovery. If not, our addiction/codependency will soon rule our lives again.

O God, keep my feet firmly planted on the Twelve-Step road.

Proverbs 15: 13–14

*A happy heart makes the face cheerful, but
heartache crushes the spirit. The discerning heart
seeks knowledge, but the mouth of a fool feeds on
folly.*

A person who is discerning seeks to grow and mature in his or her recovery, and happiness is a by-
product of that recovery. To seek happiness is
foolish, because happiness isn't something we go
out and find. Happiness, peace of mind, and serenity are the natural results of working faithfully on
recovery. Recovery teaches us to be right with God,
self, and others, and the foundation that the Steps
build in our lives will be happiness. The heartache
we knew as the result of our addiction/codepen-
dency crushed our spirits, and it was reflected in
our countenances for everyone to see.

Coming from the pit of addiction/codependency
by way of the Twelve Steps gives us the lifelong
foundation we long sought and, likewise, is reflected on our faces. What a tremendous change our
lives have experienced through the Steps. What a
difference the change is making even in the way we
look. Recovery adds years to our lives as the disease is arrested, and for many of us the change is
more than just inward. Even our speech changes.
We are mature but still young enough to enjoy our
life that has been redeemed from the pit.

*Lord, thank you for the happy face that recovery has
given me.*

Proverbs 15: 15

All the days of the oppressed are wretched, but the cheerful heart has a continual feast. Better a little with the fear of the Lord than great wealth with turmoil.

When our addiction/codependency was raging, every day was wretched. Even our best days were awful. The oppression we lived under was worse than the oppression with which Pharaoh bound the children of Israel. Addiction/codependency is like being in prison with the place of confinement growing tighter and smaller every day until the life is at last squeezed from us.

The Twelve Steps begin to push the bars back, and as we become aware that we can actually breathe again, hope begins to return, our hearts begin to experience cheerful, positive emotions, and we begin to look forward to each new day. The farther we get from the oppressive bondage we once knew, the more we experience the joy of freedom, and we can eat of that feast every day, all day.

The maturity of recovery helps us enjoy to the fullest all the areas where we are able to experience recovery, not just freedom from the drug or relationship. Recovery is a journey, but on this journey there is never a need for rationing the good things we experience.

God, you have brought me from a prison where even breath was rationed into a freedom where there is plenty.

Proverbs 15: 20–21

A wise son brings joy to his father, but a foolish man despises his mother. Folly delights a man who lacks judgment, but a man of understanding keeps a straight course.

What parent is happy when his or her child is choosing a rebellious, hurtful course in life? If our children are on the road to addiction/codependency we do everything possible to wake them up, to encourage them to see the folly of their ways. It is a wise child who listens, evaluates, and then chooses the straight course. Our Father is saddened by our choice of pathways and he does much to bring our attention to the foolishness of our lifestyle. It is easy for us to listen, ignore, and then continue pursuing the road to destruction. Many of us rejected the wisdom of our heavenly Father for years before we finally listened. It was with tender mercy that our Father allowed us to come to the end of ourselves and encouraged us to change directions into a straight path.

Lord, thank you for your continual process of change and growth.

Proverbs 15: 27–28

A greedy man brings trouble to his family, but he who hates bribes will live. The heart of the righteous weighs its answers, but the mouth of the wicked gushes evil.

Pre-recovery descriptions of addiction/codependency would always have to include the adjectives *greedy* and *selfish*. Our lives were out of control yet so controlled by our addiction/codependency that everyone in our circle of significant people experienced trouble. Greed can lead us into several manifestations of trouble.

As we mature in recovery, we find that our focus most naturally shifts from introspection to others, and we become more concerned and sensitive to their needs. As we recover, we are less likely to overlook, ignore, or minimize our inappropriate behaviors. Healing helps us to be more balanced, more aware, more assertive. Where we would have once compromised, we are more willing to confront and correct. Recovery therefore becomes a blessing not only to us but to those we rub shoulders with. We cannot be lured or enticed back to the old addictive/codependent life-style. The bribe that once would have hooked us no longer has the same power. Life, health, and the pursuit of true happiness are the natural consequences of recovery.

Lord, thank you for removing the barbs that once hooked me.

Proverbs 15: 31–32

He who listens to a life-giving rebuke will be at home among the wise. He who ignores discipline despises himself, but whoever heeds correction gains understanding.

Once we begin working the Twelve Steps and attending meetings, it becomes easier to listen to those life-giving rebukes. As our mindset begins to change, we are able to see the wisdom of those around us, where in the past we saw them as busybodies or meddlers. We begin to feel at home with those who are wise. Oftentimes we sense a family bond among those with whom we regularly attend meetings. We begin to feel comfortable with others who have struggled and are now winning. In recovery we find that discipline is one of those subjects we'd rather sidestep or ignore, but to ignore those areas we need to discipline is really a form of self-destruction. Self-hatred is often demonstrated by lack of self-discipline.

The more willing we are to be temperate, to be balanced, the more we are demonstrating a healthy self-esteem, which is a by-product of recovery. The change is obvious, not merely in the absence of addictive/codependent behavior but also in the way we feel about ourselves.

O Father, help me to become familiar with the wise.

Proverbs 16: 1

To man belong the plans of the heart, but from the Lord comes the reply of the tongue.

We enjoy making plans. We all have dreams, ambitions, and goals for how life is going to be. It is with great planning that we do something as simple as a week's vacation. Somehow it gives us a feeling of being in control or having personal power to be able to decide which route we should take, which hotel to stay in, or how long we should stay in which city.

In recovery we may also have a hidden agenda: the length of time we should be in treatment, how long this stage will last. When recovery doesn't progress the way we have planned, we begin to feel out of control, and we experience a feeling of loss of power. Those are uncomfortable feelings for those of us who are addicts/codependents. Yet those uncomfortable emotions are the very feelings that we need to embrace. To be powerless and to have given control over to the Lord is absolutely the very best place to be. When we are overcome by those feelings of powerlessness and being out of control, when we need to be doing something to feel better, the most difficult thing is to listen for God's wisdom to wait. God knows what we need.

Lord, sometimes I want to plan; other times I want simply to do—anything to feel in control. Teach me to wait and listen.

Proverbs 16: 2

All a man's ways seem innocent to him, but motives are weighed by the Lord.

As recovering addicts/codependents we can remember the days prior to recovery when we always proclaimed our innocence, when we considered ourselves helpless victims of circumstances. It is still easy to excuse ourselves, rationalize our behavior, ignore and minimize what we do or say. We can explain away hurtful remarks or actions by saying, "Well, that's just the way I am."

But as recovery progresses we become aware that behind everything we do there is often a hidden motive, an attempt to be in control, to manipulate. The Lord, the Twelve Steps, our support groups, and our sponsors help us to face the subconscious motivation behind our behavior. To see the way we have deceived ourselves into thinking we're OK is astounding. Truth that sets us free often makes us uncomfortable. We see the reality of what we have done. Facing those hidden motives and understanding those subconscious, automatic responses can be a first step in changing the old habit patterns. That begins our walk in freedom and continues our journey into wholeness.

O Lord, please continue to expose the hidden motives behind what I think is innocent.

Proverbs 16: 3

*Commit to the Lord whatever you do, and your
plans will succeed.*

Solomon reminds us once more that we must continually turn our lives and wills over to God. Every
area of our lives, not just the areas directly related to
recovery, must be given over to him. The plans we
have made, the goals we have set, the destinations
we have chosen can succeed only if we have con-
sulted the author of recovery—God.

Now, this doesn't mean that we just run the
plans by him and he gives an OK. It means that we
give him permission to change everything. It means
that we have laid those plans on the altar, taken our
hands off, moved away from the altar, and stand
ready to receive from God whatever he gives.

What a state of powerlessness, what an intense
emotion of being out of control. Yet God wants for
each of us that which will facilitate our healing, that
which promotes our recovery. This lesson continues to come to us because this seems to be the area
where we struggle the most—allowing him to direct
our lives and our recovery.

Father, teach me that I can trust my plans to you.

Proverbs 16: 4–5

*The Lord works out everything for his own
ends—even the wicked for a day of disaster. The
Lord detests all the proud of heart. Be sure of this:
They will not go unpunished.*

In recovery we eventually learn the wisdom that
God is in control. Much of our personal turmoil and
pain is simply the result of our "king baby" thinking. When we stay on the thrones of our lives, we
struggle with emotions and experience overwhelming storms. When we exert our wills over God's
plans, we always find ourselves on the losing end.
God is God, and the sooner we get off the thrones
of our lives, the sooner we experience peace of mind
and contentment.

God has a plan for each of our lives, a course for
each individual's recovery. As with Adam of old,
the question is presented to us: Will we allow God
to be God? Will we continually turn our lives and
wills over to him or will we continue to struggle to
bring about our plans and achieve our own goals?
God knew the day we started toward addiction/co-
dependency, and he knew the day we would turn to
him for help. Even then his love reached out to us.
Even when we chose to dig deeper into the pit of
destruction, his heart longed for us. And he waited,
knowing that we would need him. When we did, he
was there with the plan of recovery.

*O God, thank you for planning the way out of
addiction/codependency.*

Proverbs 16: 6

Through love and faithfulness sin is atoned for;
through the fear of the Lord a man avoids evil.

What a mess we managed to make during our addiction/codependency days. Our lives became tangled messes, and to untangle them would have been quite like unscrambling scrambled eggs. The disease of addiction/codependency often leads us into deep sin, and with sin comes guilt and condemnation and then hopelessness and finally death.

No wonder God's heart aches when he sees the path we have chosen. Knowing the terminal illness of addiction/codependency, he lovingly and faithfully made a way of escape for us. It's almost too good to be true, but our God made atonement for the effects of the disease of addiction/codependency and has released us not only from the bondage but from our guilt, shame, and feelings of unworthiness. How wonderful that God can look past the mess and see us and love us. His greatest pleasure is to redeem us from the pit and to restore our dignity as persons.

Getting to really know God will help us avoid trouble in the future. It is our respect for him and our appreciation for his plan of recovery that gives us courage to keep making those steps, to keep walking away from the failures of the past into the promise of recovery.

Father, thank you for being willing to unscramble the
mess I created during my addiction/codependency.

Proverbs 16: 7

When a man's ways are pleasing to the Lord, he
makes even his enemies live at peace with him.

Only the God of recovery could make our ways
pleasing to him. We, because of our addiction/code-
pendency, were controlled by something much
greater than our willpower and had at last to surrender to our powerlessness. At first we felt tremendous fear as the enemy of addiction/codependency
raged against us. Yet we continued to depend completely on God and his will for our recovery.
Eventually the storm began to subside. We could
rest in the peace and safety of God's gift of recovery. Even the enemy of addiction/codependency
cannot disturb the serenity that walking in God's
will brings about in our lives.

To begin the day with the first three Steps, to
practice Steps Four through Nine during the day,
and to end the day with Steps Ten and Eleven will
definitely make our ways pleasing to the Lord. This
style of living is practicing these principles in all
our affairs. Recovery is a continuing life-style, but
it is also a daily life-style, not a goal we reach but a
change of living that guarantees our success.

O Lord, thank you for taming the enemy of
addiction/codependency.

Proverbs 16: 8

Better a little with righteousness than much gain with injustice.

Realizing the hope that recovery brings and experiencing the higher self-esteem that results from recovery gives us great feelings of serenity and contentment. As God heals us and we work the Steps, we become aware of the joy of living. Little things become important, insignificant things become paramount. Flowers growing by the roadside, trees growing out of rocks, busy ants, and singing birds take on new meanings. We are able to appreciate the everydayness and see the glory of God's world as our recovering eyes open and focus. Little did we know how much life we were missing in our consumed state of addiction/codependency. Before recovery we hardly noticed even the major things of life. Even holidays were lost in the maze of our pain.

How different now—how precious life has become. Serenity helps us slow our busy pace to smell the flowers, watch the birds, hear the sounds of life, and rejoice that the little things in life have been restored to us. Recovery is life and health insurance with fringe benefits.

Father, thank you for restoring the little things in life.

Proverbs 16: 9

In his heart a man plans his course, but the Lord determines his steps.

How like children we are. In all our great plan making, God is always guiding our steps. As children learn to walk holding tightly to Daddy's fingers, he gently but firmly guides us. Our plan may have been to cross a dangerous place, but our wise parent took us around the danger spot. Our weak, unstable baby steps were supported by the loving and strong hand of our parent.

Recovery is much like that. We see the destination and we begin the journey, and in our ignorance and innocence we think we know best how to arrive at our destination. Behind it all is the Father of recovery, who is gently but firmly directing us, opening this door, closing that avenue. When we realize this, it is easier to relax when obstacles block our way. We know that God is in charge, and we can just wait for the next move.

Children eventually get stronger, and their steps are no longer unsure. They may try to run ahead. When this happens to us in recovery, we are setting ourselves up for a detour. Allowing God to direct is always the easier, more direct route that ensures recovery.

Lord, direct my path and help me depend on your guidance.

Proverbs 16: 16–17

How much better to get wisdom than gold, to choose understanding rather than silver! The highway of the upright avoids evil; he who guards his way guards his life.

In our materialistic culture, desiring wisdom or understanding more than gold or silver would be sheer folly. Before recovery we may have felt the same way, but when we begin living free of addiction/codependency, we find that wealth isn't everything. As we learn and heed the instruction given and incorporate it into our lives, we become wiser and our understanding of what is important changes. Our focus changes, and the definition of a fulfilled life changes from the temporal to the eternal. Money and things are temporary; recovery and serenity are forever. When we stop and look at the difference in the light of forever, wisdom and understanding that will change our lives win hands down. There is no comparison. This kind of wisdom helps us avoid the evil trap that once we would have fallen into so easily. The understanding that we gain through recovery is a safeguard for our way, protecting us from deadly pitfalls. The worldly concept of wealth doesn't matter after all, because we are involved in an eternal purpose.

Father, teach me what is important as I walk the road of recovery.

Proverbs 16: 18

Pride goes before destruction, a haughty spirit before a fall. Better to be lowly in spirit and among the oppressed than to share plunder with the proud.

Solomon never lets up on some topics. Pride seems to be one of them. Selfish ambition can get us into trouble in short order because we have taken the focus of our lives away from God and his plan of recovery. Once more we have taken on directorship of our lives, and unless there is a course correction we will find ourselves falling. To be lowly in spirit requires meekness, the realization that we cannot run our lives or our recovery. To admit complete dependence upon God keeps us lowly in spirit. One thing the Twelve Steps help us with is the problem of pride. Each Step reminds us that we cannot handle life, recovery, or relationships alone. What a pride breaker. Yet from the brokenness can spring forth a healthy understanding of our need for others and our responsibility to others. Sometimes it is a real "downer," but sometimes we need to be down on the terra firma of real life in order to continue recovery. As difficult as the lessons that crush pride are to accept, they really are stepping-stones to wholeness.

God, help me be willing to allow you to remove all pride, self-sufficiency, and haughtiness.

Proverbs 16: 20–21

Whoever gives heed to instruction prospers, and blessed is he who trusts in the Lord. The wise in heart are called discerning, and pleasant words promote instruction.

Learning to heed is very important in the life-style of recovery as we hear and act upon instructions given through our Twelve Steps or sponsors. To take to heart what is being shared by others helps us to avoid common pitfalls. Rebellion is an indication of an unteachable heart, but those who have learned to heed become truly wise.

We learn to discern as we are taught the value of Twelve-Step living. As we mature in the ways of recovery, we may also learn to instruct others with words of inspiration and hope rather than words of criticism, discouragement, or nagging. When we learn how to verbalize with pleasant words, we help those we are trying to instruct and train to be receptive. It is human nature to turn off those who nag, whine, or yell, even when what they are saying is true or necessary. If the same message is given to us in a pleasant tone of voice, we willingly receive it. Learning to listen is important to our recovery, and learning to share the message properly, in a positive way, is equally important.

O Lord, give me ears that heed and a voice and attitude that convey the message of recovery to others.

Proverbs 16: 22

*Understanding is a fountain of life to those who
have it, but folly brings punishment to fools.*

To understand the Twelve Steps, to understand that
these Steps are spiritual and scriptural, and to inte-
grate them into our lives produce a fountain of life
for us. Recovery is a life-giving source for those of
us who were once bound by addiction/codepen-
dency, and we know the power of the Twelve Steps
to free us. On the other hand, if we do not live by the
principles we have learned, we will fall back into
the folly of our addiction/codependency and will
reap the consequences and punishment of that folly.

The wisdom of recovery is a daily way of life; it is
a growing process that we continue throughout our
lives. Recovery begins when we realize that we are
powerless over our disease of addiction/codepen-
dency. But that is merely the beginning. There is so
much more to the plan of recovery. The depth of the
Steps reaches beyond just our addiction/codepen-
dency. Truly the Steps become a fountain of life, a
blessing to every area of our lives.

*Father, help me understand how many areas of my life
the Twelve Steps touch.*

Proverbs 16: 25

There is a way that seems right to a man, but in the end it leads to death.

Many recovering people have no problem remembering the ways they were traveling before recovery. For some it is a tale of horror, for others it is the story of a slow descent into hell, and for most of us it was a way that we would have defended as right, even to death. How blind our addiction/codependency made us to the truth. Addiction/codependency robbed us of much that was precious, but we could not see it until a crisis jolted us awake. Even being in the crisis may not have placed us in the frame of mind to seek help or recovery, but red flags warning us of danger were going up everywhere.

God intercepted our way and opened our eyes. People in Twelve-Step programs reached out and encouraged us to choose life by choosing recovery. It may not have been an easy task to get us on the road to life, but finally we changed directions.

Once, our destination was death; now it is life. What a gift those twelve simple steps are, what a life changer they have been to so many of us.

God, keep me aware of anything that would lead me back to the ways of death.

Proverbs 16: 26

The laborer's appetite works for him; his hunger drives him on.

How easy it would be just to give up the journey to recovery we have undertaken. Some days the journey seems impossible and we simply want to stop. But like the laborer's hunger that drives him to keep working, our fear of relapse has a tendency to keep us moving forward, even on impossible days. The threat of going back helps us hold on, as we remember this pit from which God redeemed us. Seeing someone else struggle with the temptation to go back into addiction/codependency helps us see how much we value the steps we have taken.

So our fear of relapse can work for us, encouraging us on our way. Our hunger for freedom, life, and serenity causes us to attend another meeting, reach out to another struggler, reach out to God, confess our shortcomings—whatever our plan of recovery involves. Freedom is worth whatever price we must pay. Slowly, day by day, we maintain the way of life we call recovery. Practicing these principles in every area of our lives will bring the same positive results that recovery has brought to our addiction/codependency. The Steps coupled with the hunger for freedom assures recovery work.

O Lord, make my hunger for recovery ravenous.

Proverbs 17: 1

Better a dry crust with peace and quiet than a house full of feasting with strife.

Peace and *quiet* are simply other words for our familiar word *serenity*. Addiction/codependency kept us in a perpetual state of chaos, and it is a blessed relief to enjoy serenity. Somehow this proverb brings to remembrance the deliciousness of peace in a world filled with noise, fuss, and strife. To be at peace with God, with oneself, with others, and with nature is so important.

As we continue maturing in our recovery, we become aware that there are some things we will not—no, cannot—live without. Peace and quiet become all important, and we can live and let live. Somehow it doesn't seem so important to be the winner of the argument, and we are able to accept what we cannot change. Things that at one time seemed so important are laid aside, while the things that are vital to serenity are held tightly. In comparison to life without peace and quiet, we find that having less really isn't such a big deal after all. One of the wonderful side effects of recovery is the beautiful sense of rest we enjoy as our bodies, souls, and spirits begin healing through the wisdom of the Twelve Steps.

God, you have given me peace and quiet; teach me to enjoy it.

Proverbs 17: 3

The crucible for silver and the furnace for gold,
but the Lord tests the heart.

As recovering addicts/codependents we may find
ourselves in some situations we would rather avoid.
We do all we know to do: we contact our sponsor,
we journal, we pray, we meditate, we attend a meeting, and we rehearse the steps, to no avail.
Remember the voice that would interrupt our fa-
vorite program on radio or TV: "This is a test"?
Sometimes as we gain maturity in our recovery, we
will hear that old familiar phrase: "This is a test."
Why do we even need tests? To show ourselves,
others, and the enemy that we have not merely ac-
cumulated knowledge, we have assimilated that
knowledge, and it has become wisdom. Only when
difficult times come can we prove the solidity of our
recovery. Only as we face difficult situations will
we know that these steps really are changing us.

Tests are just that—tests. They come, they evaluate our growth, leave us with a passing grade or
more homework to do, and then they are gone, until
the next time. Some tests we know are coming,
some are surprise quizzes, but either way they can
truly measure our growth and success in recovery.

O Lord, help me be ready when the tests come.

Proverbs 17: 9–11

He who covers over an offense promotes love,
but whoever repeats the matter separates close
friends. A rebuke impresses a man of discernment
more than a hundred lashes a fool. An evil man is
bent only on rebellion; a merciless official will
be sent against him.

Our Twelve Steps contain a rather risky step—con-
fessing to God, ourselves, and another human being
the exact nature of our wrongs. We know God won't
faint, nor will he share our offense with someone
else; therefore, he is safe. We certainly won't share
our ugliness with anyone else—we are safe, but to
risk with another person is frightening. One thing
Twelve Steppers have learned is the importance of
confidentiality. We cannot continue our healing
until we are able to trust someone with the worst
about ourselves, and yet we cannot bear the thought
of another rejection. Because each of us has things
we are deeply ashamed of, it behooves us to cover
the other person's offense, to hold in confidence the
things entrusted to us by one who is also willing to
risk. To remember that it is only by the grace of God
that we haven't done some of the things that have
been confessed to us, to be able to trust someone
with the depths of ourselves, and to know they will
cover our sin is so healing. Somehow it seems to

confirm God's love, acceptance, and forgiveness, freeing us to leave the past behind and become all that God created us to be.

Father, please help me cover the sins of others who trust me to hear their Fifth Step.

Proverbs 17: 12–13

Better to meet a bear robbed of her cubs than a
fool in his folly. If a man pays back evil for good,
evil will never leave his house.

Even as we walk in the maturity of recovery and
become wise about life, there will be people who
can hurt our feelings, if we allow it. No matter how
good we feel we are doing with relationships, there
will be some relationships that fall apart in spite of
our efforts. Everyone with whom we are in relationship is not recovering, and when we come in contact
with those who are not working their program we
may feel the results.

It takes more than just leaving off the drug of
choice, be it chemical or relational, to constitute recovery. Our response and our reaction to other people's hatefulness or impatience is a good gauge of
the maturity of our recovery. We would have the
good sense to run from a bear who had been robbed
of her cubs, but we will try to tackle and change the
opinion or life-style of "a fool" who has no intention
of following our advice. Maturity lets us walk away
with our dignity as a person still intact and the other
person's feelings about himself or herself still OK.
We cannot change "the fool," so we must accept and
detach, live and let live, and get out of the line of
fire. Of course, if we are "the fool," we can work on
ourselves, changing the things we can change.

O God, give me grace to get out of the way of those
who would hurt my recovery.

Proverbs 17: 17

A friend loves at all times, and a brother is born for adversity.

We who are living the Twelve Steps know the camaraderie of others who are also in Twelve-Step programs. Truly these brothers and sisters in recovery were born for adversity. Who else, besides God, can hear the story of our addiction/codependency and still love us? Who else would sit with us on a bad night and help us make it through the storms and rocky places? Who else could point out blind spots and areas of denial with such care? Who would know when we are avoiding the issue and call us on it? These fellow travelers are truly shining lights who have walked before us, who walk beside us, and who walk behind us, nudging us along should we need it. Because they too have been down the dark alley of addiction/codependency, they know the pitfalls, games, and rationalizations we use. These friends love us with a tough love that helps us face ourselves and yet put loving arms around us when we weep over the failures we are. These friends in recovery are truly gifts that our Father placed in our lives to make recovery just a little bit easier to handle.

O Lord, thank you for friends who understand recovery.

Proverbs 17: 22

A cheerful heart is good medicine, but a crushed spirit dries up the bones.

Indeed our spirits were crushed by our addiction/codependency. Our drug of choice consumed the very breath we breathed. Emotions, spirit, and health suffered. During our days of addiction/codependency there was little to be cheerful about. Depression and insane mood swings controlled our lives. Even in the earlier stages of recovery we may have been swept under the avalanche of emotions we experienced.

As recovery becomes our life-style, emotions begin to stabilize. But because we were so chaotic for so long, we don't develop cheerful hearts just naturally; they must be carefully planned and nurtured. The results are joy, laughter, and hope.

Humor is of absolute necessity in recovery. To laugh at ourselves can lift our spirits. Our bodies actually produce chemical changes when we laugh. Keeping our minds on encouraging and uplifting things as much as possible also helps promote cheerfulness. Cheerful hearts are good medicine not only for ourselves but also for those around us. Give yourself a laugh break today.

Father, teach me to laugh at life as often as possible.

Proverbs 17: 27–28

A man of knowledge uses words with restraint,
and a man of understanding is even-tempered.
Even a fool is thought wise if he keeps silent,
and discerning if he holds his tongue.

Everyone—not just those in recovery—could benefit from the wisdom of this passage. Perhaps the wiser we become, the less we feel the need to talk. The need to impress others fades when we are truly self-accepting, and wisdom does seem to bring acceptance. Even acceptance of others is the fruit of knowledge and wisdom. We can allow others to have an opinion that differs from ours. We can hear others say things that are even incorrect and feel not the slightest need to correct them. That is maturity. How much less complicated life becomes as we grow and mature in our attitude of acceptance. How amazing that we can allow even our children the freedom of thinking differently from us.

As we relax while we continue to recover, we realize that we do not have the ability to control anyone's words but our own. As we let go of the need to talk others into thinking the way we do, we find that our words become fewer. Recovery teaches us many things about relationships, and correcting this one thing will bring health into our relationships.

O Lord, please muzzle my mouth.

Proverbs 18: 1

An unfriendly man pursues selfish ends; he defies all sound judgment.

Addiction/codependency definitely caused us to pursue completely selfish ends. Most of the time we lacked judgment. In the beginning of recovery it may seem that we are still selfish. Not so. We must exercise self-care and protect our recovery at all costs. Family may not understand, friends may not comprehend, others may be critical, but we must pursue recovery. After the first several months, when recovery is well established, then we can begin to find balance in our lives. Learning to bring balance to meetings, Twelve Steps, sponsors, families, and social and spiritual life can be tricky, but it is possible. We learn how to incorporate the best of both worlds. The "continuing" steps become part of our daily life, and we do mature and grow as we work them. We learn to appreciate the sound judgment of others and no longer feel the need to defy the wisdom of others in order to feel important. God is indeed developing character within us.

Lord, help me know the difference between selfish ends and self-care.

Proverbs 18: 2–3

A fool finds no pleasure in understanding but delights in airing his own opinions. When wickedness comes, so does contempt, and with shame comes disgrace.

At one time we were fools; we couldn't understand why life was so complicated and we felt no restraint in sharing our opinions. The result of our addiction/codependency was shame and disgrace. But that was before we began actively recovering from our addiction/codependency. Isn't it amazing that twelve simple scripturally based steps can be used to turn a life around completely? Our inner being greedily and hungrily searches for books, tapes, seminars, meetings that give us a better understanding of our disease and recovery. We desire the knowledge that will help us continue our journey to freedom. As we've grown in our recovery, we have learned to develop the art of listening to others, even when their opinions differ from ours. That is the result of learning to be slow to speak and swift to hear. Each day as we live sober, free from addiction/codependency, the shame and disgrace fade and we are more able to forgive ourselves. As recovery matures, we develop a balanced sense of confidence, not cocky, not wimpy, but we come to know our God-given strengths and our limitations, and we accept them.

Father, deliver me from my own foolishness.

Proverbs 18: 6–7

A fool's lips bring him strife, and his mouth invites a beating. A fool's mouth is his undoing, and his lips are a snare to his soul.

Who was our worst enemy during our days of addiction/codependency? What kept us in trouble more than any one thing? Besides the disease of addiction/codependency our mouths cause us the most trouble.

Strife in our relationships usually begins with our words. Our tongue can be the undoing of our life. How often do the words we speak snare us and begin the emotions churning? What comes out of our hearts through our mouths tells us what is truly within the treasure of our beings. Our growing recovery is often manifested by a change in our words, speech, meditations. The new length that has been added to our once short fuse can also be an indication that recovery is changing us from the inside out. It's good to know that there is a purpose, a reason for recovery to take such a long time. Recovery isn't a surface fix or a patch on our lives. It is a complete restructuring, a restoration from the ground up. So as the changes happen they are usually evident through the words of our mouths.

Father, change my heart, and may others see the change through my speech.

Proverbs 18: 9

*One who is slack in his work is brother to one
who destroys.*

Addiction/codependency blinds us to anything
else because it seems to be the largest part of living. If we could just get this problem solved, then
there would be plenty of time for other matters. As
we enter the world of the recovering, there is work
to do, and we have to continue doing our part or we
will destroy the recovery we have enjoyed. Our
work may involve being faithful to our meetings
when we are down, tired, or angry. At those times
we want to stop working. But if we give in, we're
in trouble. Our work may involve calling our sponsor and talking through some issue we'd rather
bury. It may mean calling another recovering person when we feel tempted. We have work to do in
our recovery, and no one else can do it for us. Only
we can make the Steps. Only we can be obedient.
When we are faithful and do our part, recovery just
naturally happens.

*Lord, help me be faithful to do the work that is
required of me to recover.*

Proverbs 18: 10

The name of the Lord is a strong tower; the
righteous run to it and are safe.

What a wonderfully comforting thought that we in
recovery have access to the strong tower that the
name of the Lord provides. On those days when
emotions are unstable, during those stormy times or
rocky ways, we have a place of protection, security,
and safety. When something overwhelms us, we can
run into the safety of the name of the Lord. We can
snuggle deeply into the safety, warmth, and security
of our Father's arms. Our Father is never too busy
for us; no one is ever more important to him; no
problem is too big or small for his attention. The
greatest thing of all is that he wants us to come; he
makes himself completely available to us, like a
nursing mother makes herself available to her child.
Whenever we are hurting, afraid, tired, or lonely,
he welcomes us into his shelter. We can rest, refresh
ourselves, and find whatever we need to be able to
continue the journey.

Father, thank you for the safe place of rest that
your name provides.

Proverbs 18: 12

Before his downfall a man's heart is proud, but humility comes before honor.

Before we bottomed out, we were so confident, so sure of ourselves, but when our addiction/codependency took us to the end of ourselves, we came to be sure only of our powerlessness. Such a rude awakening was painful, to say the least. The bottom for most of us was so ugly, so painful that not one shred of confidence was left in us. Stripped naked by our addiction/codependency, we had nowhere to go but upward toward the journey of recovery.

For most of us, humility is a painful place. Yet only when we arrive at that place can the healing begin. Recovery restores our sense of dignity as persons, our self-esteem, and our hope. True humility brings us true honor. No one wants to go through the pain, failure, and disappointment that breaks our human pride, yet we don't change until we have endured the shame of the bottom. Being in touch with our powerlessness and our need for the God of recovery brings us to the decision that we have to reach out to him. He reaches back in such a loving way that we feel loved unconditionally and accepted as we are.

Lord, thank you for the pain of defeat that brought me to the brokenness that began my recovery.

Proverbs 18: 13

He who answers before listening—that is his folly and his shame.

As recovering people, we need to develop the art of listening. Because so many of us were poor listeners before we began recovery, we may find it difficult to be attentive listeners now. Too often we jump in to answer when we haven't even heard with our heart what is being said. This is true whether or not we are recovering from addiction/codependency. How often do we wait eagerly for the speaker to draw a breath so we can jump in with what we want to say?

To listen means we involve our entire being, our attention, our eyes, our body, our spirit, and our emotions with the one who is speaking. We keep our mind on the words being spoken and not on formulating our answer. To listen to others is a simple way of loving someone. To speak and to have someone who will listen is such a rare thing. Recovering people need to be heard, their stories need to be cherished as our own. As recovering people, we can further the process of discipline in our lives by training ourselves to listen. After all, listening is a beautiful indication of maturity.

O Lord, give me the ability to not only listen, but to hear.

Proverbs 18: 14

A man's spirit sustains him in sickness, but a crushed spirit who can bear?

Many addicts/codependents found their way into addiction/codependency because their spirits had been deeply wounded as children. We understand the concept of addiction/codependency as being a disease. Therefore it is not difficult to understand that addiction/codependency may not easily be thrown off. If our spirits are crushed when our physical immune systems are down, we are more vulnerable to disease. Likewise, when our human spirits are crushed, we are more at risk for emotional problems and maladies. The human spirit gives us the ability to handle disease, to withstand it, and to recover from it.

Our Father desires to heal our wounded, crushed, and broken spirits. He planned for Jesus to touch the crushed spirit and to heal the broken heart just as much as he freed people from sin. Indeed, our Father is the God of recovery. He understands the brokenness that may have led us into our addiction/codependency, and he desires to heal and strengthen the crushed, wounded spirit. Recovery is restoration. Since the Twelve Steps are spiritual steps, our spirit will respond positively.

Father, thank you for your concern that my entire being experience wholeness.

Proverbs 18: 19

An offended brother is more unyielding than a fortified city, and disputes are like the barred gates of a citadel.

Who among us has not been deeply hurt and offended by someone we respect? At those times our unhealthy, nonrecovering part may throw a wall up to protect us from further pain. We, likewise, have hurt and offended others and have seen a wall instantly fortify the other person's heart. To get into disputes and arguments with others is usually counterproductive.

In recovery we need openness, vulnerability, and honesty. When walls come between us and another person, it becomes very difficult to touch spirit to spirit. The Fifth Step, of necessity, requires that openness with at least one other human being. We need people in our lives. When the unyielding, fortified city has been built, how can we dismantle the bricks? Step Nine gives a mandate—to make amends. Sometimes admitting that we were wrong begins the process of bringing the wall down. If too many "I'm sorrys" have caused the person to be leery, then action is needed. It wouldn't even hurt to ask the person how we can restore the relationship. Recovery teaches us not only good spiritual concepts but how to have a life well lived.

Father, lest I offend someone, help me to be sensitive.

Proverbs 19: 2–3

It is not good to have zeal without knowledge,
nor to be hasty and miss the way. A man's own
folly ruins his life, yet his heart rages against the
Lord.

Solomon's wisdom in the Proverbs is teaching us
recovery principles that bring us maturity. Many
times we can become so excited about something
that we run off in our zeal without having enough
knowledge to be helpful. Proverbs adds the wisdom that we need. The psalms comfort us and encourage our recovery on those difficult days. The
proverbs help us deal with self. Dealing with our
addiction/codependency was only one facet of recovery. Proverbs takes us a step further to deal with
those character flaws and the roots of our addic-
tion/codependency. As we became clean through
the psalms, we now become mature through the
proverbs. Solomon continues to help us face ourselves without the buffer of excuses. By seeing our
true human nature, we can allow God to change us,
not just repair us. Painful as it is, seeing our true
selves is really the only way to maintain a life-style
of recovery. We must grow or we begin to die.

Father, please add to my zeal the knowledge needed to
mature my recovery.

Proverbs 19: 8

He who gets wisdom loves his own soul; he who cherishes understanding prospers.

The wisdom of recovery is a wonderful tool to ensure a balanced life. We who were once struggling with our addiction/codependency have learned to work the steps, and sober living has become a joyful experience. Recovery began with faltering, unstable steps; but the more steps we make, the more stable they become. Recovery is one area in which getting wisdom proves we are loving ourselves in a healthy way. Our entire life prospers when we cherish knowledge, understanding, and wisdom. Wisdom is growth, maturity, and progress, and it is ongoing. Wisdom, like recovery, is not a goal to attain but a style of living we adopt. Doctors must continue to learn. For them wisdom is a continuing process. Teachers know the importance of going back to school periodically to update their knowledge. For them wisdom becomes an ongoing process. Our recovery will stalemate unless we continue to learn about our disease, about our responses, about our relationships and life in general. Maybe recovery could be considered our continuing education.

Father, teach me to cherish understanding as you process it into wisdom.

Proverbs 19: 11

A man's wisdom gives him patience; it is to his glory to overlook an offense.

The writer of Proverbs spends a great deal of time dealing with offenses, words, and reactions. Patience isn't a virtue many people are born possessing. Most of us develop it through difficult times with difficult people. In recovery we learn the importance of living and letting the other live. We are taught how to discriminate between the things we can change and the things we cannot change. Wisdom helps us to rest in the knowledge that we can't change anyone else. As we accumulate our clean time without the influence of our drugs or relationships, we begin to see the dynamics of relationships. It's amazing how the Twelve Steps, practiced in all our affairs, bring us to maturity and mellow us. Things that once ticked us off don't seem to have the same power in our lives. Patience becomes second nature, and we can overlook many of the things that once bent us out of shape. Once more we are able to enjoy the wonderful joy of serenity as we choose the proper response and decide not to allow anyone or anything to disturb our peace.

Father, please give me the grace to overlook those offenses that once demanded a response.

Proverbs 19: 22

What a man desires is unfailing love; better to be poor than a liar.

Each of us is born into this world with a deep desire and need for unfailing love. To be loved in spite of ourselves and to be loved for ourselves is a dream come true. Codependents feel called to love in such a way and find problem situations just the perfect opportunity. Both addicts and codependents are hurting, and both need this unfailing love. In actuality the codependent tries to stop the throbbing pain by loving too much, by enabling, by rationalizing the behavior of the loved one. Rescuing is another way we have of "loving unconditionally." In reality this is still our unhealthy way of trying to fix our pain, by healing the pain of someone else.

The wisdom of recovery tells us that no human love is strong enough or healthy enough to heal either ourselves or someone else. Facing that truth dispels the illusion, and we are able to learn to love in a healthy way. Much of the wisdom we learn in recovery frees us to become mature people who know how to balance love and self-care.

O Lord, teach me to lean on your unfailing love for myself and for the ones I thought I could love enough to make well.

Proverbs 19: 23

The fear of the Lord leads to life. Then one rests content, untouched by trouble.

As Christians in recovery, we are comforted by the knowledge that the Twelve Steps are biblically based. In the initial Steps we came to believe that God could restore us to sane living. Those Steps began the journey to life and health. The more we practice those Steps, the more we come to depend on the Lord for guidance, wisdom, and insight and the more we experience life. For so long our addiction/codependency robbed us of life and contentment, and we were surrounded by trouble. The contrast is remarkable as we see the Twelve Steps bring order to our chaos and peace to our turmoil. Only God could bring peace to our troubled being and health to our body. Turning our lives and wills over to the care of God was the starting point, the beginning, but as we continue to work that Step diligently, we find our trust level just naturally brings us peace. Indeed the fear, the awe, the knowledge of God leads us to life, and we are able to be content and fulfilled. What a difference recovery and the wisdom it brings can make in our lives.

God, help me come to know you in a way that brings me to life.

Proverbs 20: 3

It is to a man's honor to avoid strife, but every
fool is quick to quarrel.

Addiction/codependency left us very vulnerable
to strife and quarreling. Our ability to deal with conflict had been deeply impaired, and we either
stuffed our anger or exploded it on those around.

The wisdom of recovery teaches us how important it is to process negative emotions appropriately.
As we learn this communication skill, it becomes
easier to avoid strife. As we mature in our recovery,
we realize that peace and serenity are quickly lost
when we quarrel and argue. It becomes easier to
allow those whose opinions differ from ours to have
their opinions without our feeling the slightest need
to make them think the way we do. After all, isn't
that what we are trying to do when we argue—convince the other person that we are right? The wisdom we've learned in recovery reminds us to live
and let live. What great transformation this simple
wisdom has brought into our lives.

Father, give me the courage to allow others to see
things differently than I do.

Proverbs 20: 4

A sluggard does not plow in season; so at harvest time he looks but finds nothing.

In recovery we find that we are planting for a future harvest. Our crops from our addiction/codependency days were not much to look at. Now we have a new life and a new opportunity to plant a crop of life rather than a crop of death. The wisdom of recovery reminds us that even in recovery we must prepare the soil, plant the seeds, pull the weeds, fertilize and water the crop. Otherwise there will be no harvest. In other words, as we work our program faithfully, recovery cannot help but happen. As we carefully work the Steps that involve pulling weeds, Steps Four, Five, and Six, we are ensuring a bountiful harvest. If we neglect those Steps, or any Steps, we will be disappointed in our expectation of the fruit of recovery.

Harvest is just another season to those not concerned with farming, but to the farmer, it is a time of reward for a job well done. Harvest also provides seeds for future crops, so there is an investment for the coming year. Our recovery is just like that; we get out of our program only what we are willing to put into it.

Lord, thank you for the seeds of recovery that will produce a good crop if I do my part.

Proverbs 20: 15

*Gold there is, and rubies in abundance, but lips
that speak knowledge are a rare jewel.*

What could be more beautiful than gold and rubies?
Yet to be able to speak from the storehouse of
knowledge we have attained from recovery is rarer
even than precious jewels. Each story is important,
and every time our stories are shared, someone else
receives hope from them. The similar events, the
struggles, the victories become maps for someone
else to follow. When we see someone who has felt
similar emotions and continued to recover, we feel
hope. No one can travel the Steps of recovery and
not gain tremendous wisdom. Each Step of our recovery is so important and each one builds upon
the previous one. Each individual possesses her
own wealth of wisdom, each one has that rare jewel
of his own story. Just as each story is strangely like
another, each story is unique. Our messages are full
of wisdom, direction, and insight. The recovering
person truly speaks knowledge that is worth listening to. Jewels and gold can be lost or stolen, but the
wisdom of recovery is a lifetime guarantee for
health and wholeness.

Father, teach my lips to speak knowledge.

Proverbs 21: 2

In the house of the wise are stores of choice food and oil, but a foolish man devours all he has.

Deferred gratification is an almost unheard-of thing in our society. We are the "now" generation living in the fast lane, enjoying instant life. Perhaps this lack of deferred gratification is part of the reason we became addicted/codependent. We found something that felt good, and we enjoyed the temporary absence of pain.

In the wisdom of recovery, we learn the art of waiting, of postponing, and of denying the flesh completely, if need be. We learn that temporary craving will not snuff out life and that we do not always have to have things our way. We will survive. In the development of the wisdom of recovery, we learn to save, to accumulate, and to wait. Each lesson is part of our ongoing education that assures us of daily recovery. In the days before we began recovery, we devoured everything we had and anything we could beg, borrow, or steal from anyone else. Our empty lives consumed everything trying to fill up the emptiness. Now we are full of life itself, and we can handle whatever we have to face.

Lord, help me wait when I need to wait, and give me courage to say no when I need to say no.

Proverbs 21: 21

He who pursues righteousness and love finds life, prosperity and honor.

The life-style of recovery has many fringe benefits. We have seen this in the Book of Proverbs more than once. To continue pursuing wholeness, recovery, and healthy relationships ensures that we'll experience life to the fullest, prosperity, and a deep feeling of self-worth. Our addiction/codependency had convinced us that our lives were not worth even the salt in our bread. Addiction/codependency had robbed us of far more than finances; it had stolen the very essence of life and living. We were like empty shells, hollow and lifeless.

Recovery restores us to sane *living*. Recovery does more than free us from our drugs or relationships. Recovery teaches us to live life successfully. The mature Steps of recovery lead us into more fulfilled lives. *Restoration* is another word for recovery. The God of recovery can and will restore and make new whatever has been destroyed. Recovery is a call to new life daily, new experiences and contentment, serenity, solutions to many of our problems, hope, and security. What a wonderful package the life-style of recovery offers us. It is well worth the cost.

O Lord, thank you for all the extra blessings I've experienced in the journey of recovery.

Proverbs 21: 31

The horse is made ready for the day of battle, but victory rests with the Lord.

Victory over our addiction/codependency rests with the Lord, provided we carefully follow the plan of recovery he has given us. The Twelve Steps are God's tools to help us find not just sobriety or freedom from codependency but a true understanding of him. If we gain sobriety but do not come to have a deeper and more meaningful understanding of the God of recovery, we have not truly experienced the complete victory of recovery. Our enemy had bound us hard and fast, and we struggled to get free; but the more we struggled, the deeper our bondage became. Only when we truly realized we were hopelessly bound did we give our life and will over to God and allow him to work the work of transformation in our lives.

Our Father wants to give us victory over whatever we struggle with, but he can't as long as we think we are doing a pretty good job in our own strength. So the first Step to victory is admitting defeat. Our victory rests with the Lord, therefore our victory is a settled thing. Our partnership with God and others in Twelve-Step recovery ensures victory.

Father, help me to experience the victory you desire for my life.

Proverbs 22: 1

A good name is more desirable than great riches;
to be esteemed is better than silver or gold.

Each one of us wants to be well thought of by other
people. But being codependents, we can easily give
our entire being away, trying to gain the acceptance
of others. We will move heaven and earth to make
everyone else's life work, while our life is ebbing
away. Our addiction to people will rob us if we re-
main addicted. Everyone desires to be esteemed,
and yet we most often need to esteem ourselves.

A truly good name is the manifestation of a life
well lived. Addiction/codependency had stolen our
good name, and it seemed hopeless to regain the
esteem of people. Yet look at the millions of people
who were hopelessly addicted but now make great
contributions to recovery. The books written for us
by others who are recovering touch our lives much
more deeply than the words of theory spouted by
the never addicted/codependent person. Those
who have pioneered the way for us in recovery are
the very ones who made the biggest and most em-
barrassing messes in addiction/codependency.
God, too, gives a good name and esteem to those
who diligently pursue recovery.

O God, thank you for restoring my name and esteem
through the Twelve Steps.

Proverbs 22: 3

A prudent man sees danger and takes refuge, but the simple keep going and suffer for it.

As we continue to mature in our Steps of recovery, we learn to see potential danger spots and to avoid them. We learn as recovering addicts/codependents where to set personal boundaries and how to protect ourselves when unhealthy people cross the line. Unlike our beginning Steps where we were open to everyone and everything, we learn that healthy self-care may involve saying no when it would be more comfortable to say yes. Learning to evaluate possible danger spots and people is wisdom that gives us refuge. We learn when to stop, yield, or proceed rather than being ignorant to the warning signs of relapse. In recovery we are well aware of the danger of relapse. Yet the old addictive/codependent personality can cause us to ignore the early warnings and fall back into the pit.

That is why we constantly need the reminder that we are not aiming at a goal we will one day reach and then just kick back and rest. Recovery is a continuing journey of daily Steps. The danger of relapse is real, but just as real is the security that we will not relapse as long as we take refuge in our God and the Twelve Steps.

O Lord, help me run to you when the danger of relapse threatens me.

Proverbs 22: 4

*Humility and the fear of the Lord bring wealth
and honor and life.*

Humility is the opposite of pride and selfish ambition. Fearing the Lord is the opposite of rebellion and running our lives. To develop these qualities in recovery means faithfully working Steps Six and Seven. Maturity in our recovery often comes about as the result of severe correction and discipline as we learn to allow God to remove these defects. The soul surgery is painful, yet the results are worth embracing the pain. To come to the realization that we cannot run our lives or recoveries is indeed a pride killer. To realize that we must depend on God to change us can help us draw nearer to him.

Our addiction/codependency sapped our life, health, prosperity, and relationships. It left us for dead on the highway of defeat. Recovery lifts us up, bandages the wounds, strengthens our hearts, rebuilds confidence, not in self but in God, and restores health and life. What a contrast. Recovery brings us to true humility, true respect for God and then adds prosperity, honor, and new life.

*Father, teach me the true grace of revering you and
becoming truly humble.*

Proverbs 23: 15–16

My son, if your heart is wise, then my heart will be glad; my inmost being will rejoice when your lips speak what is right.

The proverbs continue to bring us to the theme of wisdom for recovery. When our hearts are filled with wisdom, those who care are glad for us. Recovery is the wisest thing we can do. It assures us of life and serenity. Our mouths speak forth what is really in our hearts, and when our words reflect that our heart is right and recovery is happening, then others who understand recovery will rejoice.

As we continue recovering and growing in our maturity of recovery, we will be rewarded. One blessing of recovery is finding friends in the family of recovering people. We find those who cheer us on, encourage us, and inspire us because they too have walked where we walk now. Wisdom in recovery teaches us the importance of having other people who hear us and those who need us to hear them. The recovering population becomes a network of caring, supportive people who rejoice when we rejoice and weep when we weep. What a great blessing our recovering family is to our lives.

O Lord, thank you for those who listen and hear and then cheer me on.

Proverbs 23: 18

There is surely a future hope for you, and your hope will not be cut off.

What a wonderful promise! Recovery through the Twelve Steps will lead us from hopelessness into hope. How important hope is to our continuing journey of recovery. Hope keeps us making Steps when hard times come along. Hope keeps us looking for growth even when we feel we've lost ground. Hope is a cousin to faith, and we need the gift of hope. Recovery teaches us to hope again. The Twelve Steps show us that we have good things to look forward to today, but also in the future. Hope reminds us that although we are not what we would like to be, we are not where we were when we began the journey, and that God isn't finished with us yet.

As we continue to walk faithfully on the pathway of recovery, we can rest assured that this hope will not be disappointed. Our expectations of people, relationships, or even ourselves may be disappointed, but hope will not be disappointed or cut short. Hope is vital to our success, and because God is the author of this hope, we can know that all he has planted in our hearts will come to pass.

Father, thank you for the gift of hope.

Proverbs 23: 19

Listen, my son, and be wise, and keep your heart on the right path.

Most of us find it difficult to listen. Our mouth is engaged in talking far more than our ears are involved in listening. Yet listening to others, to life, and to God are the beginning of becoming wise. To listen means we open ourselves up, accepting the fact that someone else has information that may benefit us. Listening could indicate that we do not know everything, which is a pride killer. In recovery we have to continue checking the map to know that we are on the right path. If we are too busy talking, we might miss a turn and thus find the direction of our recovery altered.

But stopping to listen to others who are recovering can give us clear direction. To listen to our Father as we continue getting to know him keeps our Steps on the right path. To listen to our own bodies can warn us of impending danger if we know what to listen for. Listening to our attitudes and to self-talk can give us a feel for the direction we are going.

Lord, open my ears to listen so that I may become wise enough to stay on the right path.

Proverbs 24: 3–4

By wisdom a house is built, and through
understanding it is established; through
knowledge its rooms are filled with rare and
beautiful treasures.

Wisdom for recovery builds the house of our freedom and serenity. Our understanding of addic-
tion/codependency plus understanding the Twelve
Steps establishes our emotional healing in bedrock.
When something is established, it is there for the
duration! Recovery is proven to be the life-style that
will produce well-being in every area of our lives.
To have a house that is empty is one thing, but to
have it filled with good things that make living
more comfortable and fulfilling is another. The
growing knowledge and the continuing Steps of recovery (Steps Ten through Twelve) consistently
bring a new depth to life. The house filled with nice
furnishings is a real joy.

Continuing throughout our life to maintain freedom from addiction/codependency brings rare and
beautiful treasures that can be inherited by those
who come after us. The information we gain
through reading becomes knowledge as we apply
it to our lives, then it becomes wisdom as it becomes
part of us. The Steps were the way out, but information became wisdom as we made the Steps work
in our lives. The developing maturity of recovery
becomes like a valuable antique that increases in

value with age. We protect those rare and beautiful treasures at all costs. Likewise our recovery must be guarded at all costs.

O God, thank you for the wisdom, understanding, and knowledge that have become rare and beautiful treasures.

Proverbs 24: 5

A wise man has great power, and a man of knowledge increases strength; for waging war you need guidance, and for victory many advisers.

The only way to have power in recovery is to admit our powerlessness and turn our lives and wills over to God. We find the strength we need to face the obstacles in our pathway as we rely on God's strength. That is the true wisdom of recovery.

We do not have the ability to handle any part of our lives. The war against addiction/codependency requires that we have the guidance of those who have successfully outmaneuvered the enemy. Victory is guaranteed if we follow the advice of those who have left us the Twelve Steps. We are successful when we listen to and follow those who have been successful. The fellowship of recovering people is so important. To see the lives and hear the testimonies and to watch the obvious growth is inspirational. To rub shoulders with those who have struggled and won gives us added strength for the battles we may be facing. To see the possibility of recovery as a reality in the lives of others gives us the strength of spirit needed to continue the journey when there are some deserts to cross or some mountains to climb.

Father, thank you for the power you give me to face my powerlessness.

Proverbs 24: 13

Eat honey, my son, for it is good, honey from the comb is sweet to your taste. Know also that wisdom is sweet to your soul; if you find it, there is a future hope for you, and your hope will not be cut off.

Eating honey from the comb is sweet to the taste, and honey can give a burst of energy when our strength has been depleted. In the same way that honey is a blessing to our taste and our bodies, wisdom is sweet to the soul. As we have grown stronger in our recovery, we have learned how to handle wayward emotions by correcting our stinking thinking. We have learned simple phrases that help us turn to God when we are overwhelmed with situations. "Let go and let God"; "turn it over"; "God grant me the serenity to accept the things I cannot change"; "I am powerless over this." These are more than catchy words. They become a way of life for us.

The wisdom of recovery teaches us new methods of coping, and the result is sweet peace and serenity in place of turmoil. This wisdom helps us become stable and strong and able to withstand the storms that are bound to break over us from time to time. Wisdom becomes sweet to our soul, providing a source of strength when our emotional battery has been drained.

O Lord, truly the wisdom of recovery has turned the lemons of life into tasty lemonade.

Proverbs 24: 19

Do not fret because of evil men or be envious of
the wicked, for the evil man has no future hope,
and the lamp of the wicked will be snuffed out.

Before we began recovery we had no hope, and the
little light we had left was quickly being snuffed
out by the addiction/codependency. The future was
bleak. The darker our world became, the easier it
was to just go with the flow. Thank God for the
darkness that eventually caused us to turn to the
faith and hope of the Twelve Steps. At first in the beginning of our journey, we may have looked back
from time to time when the pain of being without
our drugs of choice/relationships was too much.
We may have thought about the relief we once
found in them, but soon enough the light exposed
that delusion. The wisdom of recovery helped us
see the lie we had once believed. There is nothing
back there to fret about and nothing to envy. Today
we have hope, peace, light, and clear direction as we
make those Steps into the healing.

Father, I thank you that recovery helps me see
addiction/codependency as it really is.

Proverbs 24: 26

An honest answer is like a kiss on the lips.

To be honest with ourselves, God, and others is a vital part of recovery. The way we once lived in denial about our disease was anything but a kiss on the lips. The pain of addiction/codependency forced us to face the truth that we were hopelessly caught in bondage. The truth stung like a slap on the face, yet we had to face the truth to get free. To face the truth of our sickness and the ruin we were experiencing was the beginning of a new life. The new life of recovery develops and matures, and we become able to face the truth about ourselves on a continuing basis as we take a daily personal inventory. There are Steps that get us on the journey, and there are Steps that focus on continuing the journey. The ability to share the truth about ourselves with God is another great Step, but to share with other earthlings is a monumental one. To be able to face the truth about where we have been and where we are now is the kiss of recovery. To no longer need to hide from ourselves, God, and others is liberating.

Lord, help me honestly answer myself, others, and you.

Proverbs 24: 27

*Finish your outdoor work and get your fields
ready; after that, build your house.*

Priorities are important in every area of life, but to
have a successful life of recovery, having priorities
in order is a must. We can't build a superstructure
until we have removed the debris and cleared the
spot. The clearing away may seem menial and boring, yet that must be accomplished first. To bring
wood, nails, or marble to the building site is mean-
ingless unless we have done first things first. Skilled
craftsmen cannot begin their part on the building
until the site is prepared, the foundation has been
laid, and the outer walls built.

In recovery we are building, and sometimes it
seems unimportant to remind ourselves that we are
still powerless. Steps One through Three are our
outdoor work, but it must be done. Then things
must be cleared away in Steps Four through Nine to
have a place ready to build. As we become more
mature in our recovery, we understand the reason
for the order of the Steps. To adults priorities make
sense; to children they are cumbersome.

*Father, give me an understanding of how my priorities
should line up.*

Proverbs 24: 30–31

I went past the field of the sluggard, past the vineyard of the man who lacks judgment; thorns had come up everywhere, the ground was covered with weeds, and the stone wall was in ruins.

To begin recovery and not progress and mature in the Steps produces a life much like the field of the sluggard or the vineyard of the man who lacks judgment. It is quite possible to abstain from our drugs of choice or unhealthy relationships and still not live sober lives. Thorns are everywhere, the ground is full of weeds, the wall is in ruins. It is not enough to begin. We must continue the journey. It is not even enough to continue; we must develop, mature, learn, and stretch beyond the comfortable.

Here again the lesson comes to us that we cannot build unless the area is prepared. If we are lazy in our recovery, we will soon be overtaken by old habits and attitudes. Weeding the garden early in the season is a good beginning, but it must continue throughout the growing season. Making a searching moral inventory is indeed a good beginning, but the continuing inventory is essential to keeping the weeds out of our recovery. The wisdom of recovery helps us develop the needed judgment to live sober lives and to enjoy the journey.

O Lord, keep me from habits and attitudes that would make me lazy in my recovery.

Proverbs 24: 32

*I applied my heart to what I observed and learned
a lesson from what I saw:*

The Book of Proverbs teaches us great truths about
the ongoing life-style of recovery. Proverbs brings
us into maturity in our lifelong use of the Twelve
Steps. Proverbs teaches us to become people of wisdom and good judgment. Proverbs teaches, but we
have a part to do; we must apply our hearts to what
we read, and we will then learn from what we see.

God can turn the messes we have made into mir-
acles through the Twelve Steps, but we must be
willing to work the Steps. For every person who is
actively recovering from addiction/codependency,
there is another who remains in bondage. Both have
the Twelve Steps available, both have meetings they
can attend, and yet one does not recover. The plain
and simple difference is that one does his or her
part, the other does not. Recovery is a daily journey
as we live those Twelve Steps, watch our stinking
thinking, and purpose in our hearts to do our part.
Recovery is hard work. Sometimes it gets boring.
But the results are wonderful.

*O God, grant me the ability and willingness to apply
my heart to the principles.*

Proverbs 25: 11

A word aptly spoken is like apples of gold in settings of silver. Like an earring of gold or an ornament of fine gold is a wise man's rebuke to a listening ear.

Learning when to speak and when to keep silent is an important aspect not only of recovery but also of relationships in general. Most of us find that we are more like bulls in a china shop than apples of gold in settings of silver. Proverbs has a great deal to say about our speech. A sign of wisdom is often how well one controls one's tongue. Knowing when and how to correct or confront requires wisdom. Sponsors know the importance of being able to say something in a way that makes it acceptable. If we turn off the one we're trying to teach, then our influence is greatly hampered. As recovering people, we want to know how to say things in a way that encourages others to listen. By the same token we want to develop the gift of listening, even when we are hearing something we'd rather not. To receive correction is a hallmark of maturity. To be able to affirm those around us is a sign of growth.

Father, give me the ability to speak words that are appropriate.

Proverbs 25: 13

Like the coolness of snow at harvest time is a
trustworthy messenger to those who send him;
he refreshes the spirit of his masters.

In our recovery process many come our way to
share a word of encouragement with us. They bring
the cool, refreshing waters when our soul is dry and
thirsty. The people who lift our spirits and encourage our recovery are those trustworthy messengers
who have gone before us and know the road we are
traveling. I believe our Father sends these people
to us as an extra blessing to our lives. We really do
need to hear the voices of those who know how
emotions can overtake us when we least expect it.
We need to hear their stories of how they made it
through this hump or that slump. We need to be reminded that this is only a phase, this is temporary,
and "this too shall pass." Just when we are most
vulnerable to falling we hear or read words that re-
vive our spirits to continue the journey and overcome the temptation to give up. We all face those
times when we need someone to remind us that recovery is a lifetime journey that leads to abundant
life.

O God, thank you for those faithful messengers who
have encouraged my recovery.

Proverbs 25: 16

*If you find honey, eat just enough—too much of
it, and you will vomit. Seldom set foot in your
neighbor's house—too much of you, and he will
hate you.*

Which of us who fight with addiction/codepen-
dency knows anything about temperance? Many of
us struggle to not become addicted to something
else even as we are learning to live without our
drugs of choice or relationships. *Balance* is a very
remote word to those of us who belong to the world
of the addicted/codependent. There never comes a
time when we can have "just enough" of the drug of
choice or relationship. Total abstinence is required.
The wisdom of recovery does help us to learn balance in other areas of our lives. We learn that to
overindulge in anything is not healthy. The Steps
of recovery keep us looking and checking up on
ourselves so that any indiscretion or overindul-
gence can be brought into balance quickly. The
weakness is there, but wisdom shows us how to
handle the weakness by admitting powerlessness
over it and turning over our lives and wills to God.
How often we have to go back to those first three
Steps tells us that we are learning the importance
of balance in our lives.

Lord, please teach me the secret of a balanced life.

Proverbs 25: 21–22

*If your enemy is hungry, give him food to eat; if
he is thirsty, give him water to drink. In doing
this, you will heap burning coals on his head,
and the Lord will reward you.*

In the Twelve Steps we are told what to do in the in-
stances of having hurt or offended someone. We
confess and make amends. But the wisdom of
Proverbs helps us also to see how to handle those
who have hurt us or who choose to be our enemies.
Steps Eight and Nine are difficult, but we who have
done the work know the release and serenity that
accompanies their completion. Possibly even more
difficult is handling those who have become es-
tranged from us and who maintain their positions
as enemies. Our flesh might easily settle for distance, punishment or open rejection. Our recovery
will not allow that, and the wisdom of recovery
says we can bless those who have hurt us. The ev-
eryday acts of feeding him if he is hungry, and giving him drink when he is thirsty are ways we can
try to bridge the gap. Even if the person refuses reconciliation, the Lord will reward us for our efforts.
Either way, we come out with maturity and with
God's blessing.

Father, teach me how to bless those who hurt me.

Proverbs 25: 25–26

Like cold water to a weary soul is good news from a distant land. Like a muddied spring or a polluted well is a righteous man who gives way to the wicked.

Solomon described in a word picture the results of recovery. In our recovery we learn how to have a balanced life, and our lives become refreshment to those around. People can drink from our lives and glean from our hearts the hope and inspiration needed to enter recovery, maintain recovery and continue recovery. Solomon's word picture is also descriptive of our lives before recovery. Truly we were like a muddied spring, offering nothing clean to drink. Relapse is also described here as a polluted well, once clean and pure, but somewhere something polluted the water. The wisdom of recovery reminds us that many struggling people have never understood the power of recovery or the strength of the Twelve Steps. They are thirsty for a drink of clear, pure water. In Step Twelve we are reminded that as we share this with others our own recovery is strengthened. Pools of water become stagnant and foul when there is no outlet. Our recovery needs the outlet of sharing with others the cool, healing streams of the Twelve Steps.

O God, help me always to have clean water to offer those who are thirsty.

Proverbs 26: 14

Without wood a fire goes out; without gossip a quarrel dies down.

Many of us experience a blaze of hope when we first begin our recoveries. There is something exciting about getting well, about loving life instead of living the death of our addiction/codependency. The meetings, hearing others' stories, fellowshipping with other recovering people, and working the Steps all add fuel to the fire of recovery. As long as we work the Steps, recovery is guaranteed. But just as a natural fire goes out if no one continues to put wood on it, recovery fizzles out unless we keep adding the wood. When we take recovery for granted, the flame is going out. When we get lazy about attending meetings, the fire is being smothered. When we avoid our sponsor and his or her wisdom, the fire is being extinguished. We may not fall into full addiction/codependency all at once, but certainly we will not continue living sober lives.

Our relationship with recovery is too important to allow the flame to go out. Whatever it takes to rekindle the flame is worth the discomfort we experience.

O Lord, help me to continue putting wood on the fire of recovery.

Proverbs 27: 1

*Do not boast about tomorrow, for you do not
know what a day may bring forth.*

Recovery teaches us the secret of one day at a time,
and the theme is repeated in the wisdom of
Proverbs. Most of us are masters at bringing tomorrow's problems into the present by being overly concerned with what may happen or what we may face.
The wisdom that Proverbs gives us trains us to live
today and not fret about the outcome of tomorrow.
God gives us grace and strength for each day as it
comes. When we borrow the problems, we make our
burden for today heavier. So often we allow tomor-
rows to steal our todays. Learning to live one day at
a time brings us peace of mind as we work out whatever today holds and enjoy the blessings of the present. Handle today, because it's the only day for
which God provides grace. One day at a time,
twenty-four hours a day helps us unlock yesterday's
problems and keeps us from taking on the stress of
the future. Daytight compartments are the secret of
serenity. Doing our best today, depending on God
for wisdom for this day, enjoying this day, focusing
on this day, will strengthen recovery.

*Lord, teach me the secret of not borrowing
from tomorrow.*

Proverbs 27: 5–6

Better is open rebuke than hidden love. Wounds from a friend can be trusted, but an enemy multiplies kisses.

One of the most important people in our recovery is the person who loves us enough to help us face ourselves. It may be our sponsor or a special friend, but recovery is not complete without someone who can hear our Fifth Step with love and compassion and continue to correct our faults and failures. This may be the most painful part of recovery, yet we must have that correction because so often we are blind to our own ways. Each of us needs the presence of a person in our lives who will be faithful to rebuke us with care. The wounds these friends inflict always help to facilitate recovery and healing. Each one of us needs to be accountable to someone else as a matter of discipline in our recovery. These persons are blessings of God to our lives, because they correct us, encourage us, have insight into us, and know our weaknesses and still love us. Our trust is firmly planted in the love and care of these persons because they understand where we have been and accept us where we are now, but they encourage us to grow.

Father, thank you for my friend who helps me see my mistakes but doesn't give up on me because I'm not perfect.

Proverbs 27: 9

Perfume and incense bring joy to the heart, and the pleasantness of one's friend springs from his earnest counsel.

In our Twelve-Step meetings we come in contact with many people who have been on the journey longer than we have and are wiser in the ways of recovery than we are. There are Twelve-Steppers that we may laugh with, some we may share pleasant times with, but those we draw the most strength from will be those to whom we listen. Those are the friends we turn to in confusion or pain, and their wisdom shines a light on our path. Even when the counsel is not what we want to hear, we know it comes from a sincere heart that wants the best for us. Our Twelve-Step fellowships are groups of people who know the pain of addiction/codependency well and have learned the importance of sharing themselves with others. They have made a gift of love to others who struggle from time to time. Just as perfume and incense are pleasant to the smell and lift our spirits, those wise friends are precious because they are willing to walk with us on our journey, and their counsel guides us on a straight path.

O God, help me become a friend to other recovering people, and give me wise counsel for others.

Proverbs 27: 12

The prudent see danger and take refuge, but the simple keep going and suffer for it.

Wisdom teaches us prudence, and prudence helps us see danger before we fall into it. Before we were firmly established in our recovery it was easy to stray into dangerous areas or follow people who were not recovering. As we have matured in the ways of recovery, we want to protect our recovery at all costs, even when it means avoiding certain situations or people. We have learned not to get too hungry, angry, lonely, or too tired, because this is dangerous to our sobriety. At first we may have thought that slogan was a nice reminder, but as we continue to mature in the Steps, we learn the signs that say we're in dangerous territory. We learn the warning signs and heed them. Anything or anyone that causes us to compromise our progress is dangerous.

Addiction/codependency is a defeated foe as long as we stay secure in the fortress of our Twelve Steps of recovery. When we forget that this is a lifetime journey and think we don't need the discipline of the Steps, we are on the way to falling. Thank goodness we do not have to relapse, that we can see the danger and take refuge.

Lord, thank you for the safety that recovery provides.

Proverbs 27: 17

As iron sharpens iron, so one man sharpens another.

Nothing exposes the unfinished work in us quicker than another human being. Someone rubbing us the wrong way can bring up from our depths the areas still needing recovery. The early stages of recovery were basically getting clean, learning to balance self-care and other care, and remaining free of our addiction/codependency. That seemed to take all our time and energy. Recovery isn't just Twelve Steps that deal with addiction/codependency. These steps deal with life. The wisdom of recovery helps us learn how to have meaningful and successful relationships. It is important to understand that those people who are sources of irritation in our lives are instruments by which God shows us still unhealed areas. If we never had conflict, then we would be blissfully unaware of areas that still need work. The Twelve Steps encompass the whole person, our complete life. When someone sparks an overreaction within us, it is a signal that our Father is ready to remove one of these character defects.

Lord, thank you for the friends who grind away on me until I turn to you.

Proverbs 27: 19

As water reflects a face, so a man's heart reflects the man.

The Twelve Steps help to expose the defects of character and the shortcomings that need to be removed by God. Those areas that need attention are often buried deep within our subconscious. We cannot know what is in our hearts because of the defense structures of denial and avoidance. We are often surprised when something unpleasant pops out of our mouths, and we may say, "I don't know where that came from," or "That's not me." Yet the opposite is true, because from the abundance of our hearts our mouths speak. Our reactions often show us our real heart. As we continue to mature in the ways of recovery, we go deeper into the hidden areas of our subconscious.

Recovery and the Twelve Steps could really be referred to as deep cleaning. Those steps purge, burn, remove, and scrape away every character defect and every shortcoming as we continue to work the Steps. The continuing inventory keeps us open and willing to admit we're wrong, and these two facets of recovery will certainly flush any impurity of soul or spirit to the surface for removal or correction.

O God, I don't always like what I see in my heart when it is exposed. Please change me.

Proverbs 28: 1

The wicked man flees though no one pursues, but the righteous are as bold as a lion.

In the days of addiction/codependency, we often felt that everyone was out to get us. We left a path of destruction behind us, and we were often running in our paranoia. Most often we were running from having to face ourselves.

But the Twelve Steps mercifully help us to face what we are and what we have done and then restore our sense of dignity by allowing us to make amends. Eventually our shame gives way to experiencing the forgiveness of God, of those we have wounded, and then self. We can now face life with confidence, not in self but in the God of recovery. Like a child standing behind an older brother when the bully comes around, we rest in our Father's strength and his ability to handle the enemy, our addiction/codependency. The wisdom of recovery helps us become strong enough and confident enough to face ourselves, life, or whatever else we may have to face. We are no longer wimps who are afraid of everything. We are bold, and nothing frightens us.

Father, when I stand in your strength, I am not afraid.

Proverbs 28: 5

Evil men do not understand justice, but those
who seek the Lord understand it fully.

During our pre-recovery days, nothing seemed fair
to us, justice was anything but just. It seemed that
even God was against us. With minds clouded by
our addiction/codependency, we could not understand that "what goes around comes around."
Consequences seemed to be just another attempt
of life to frustrate us.

As we begin to recover, we begin to understand
through Twelve-Step living that there are just dues
that each of us must pay and amends we must be
willing to make in order to get our lives back on
track. The more we understand God and his ways,
we become aware of what real justice is and how it
works. Our understanding of justice begins to grow
and mature as our life-style of recovery matures.
At the beginning our ideas of justice may have applied to other persons, but as the childish ideas give
way to a more mature understanding, we see that
justice and fairness and retribution apply to us all.
What a wonderful discovery to realize that we are
not victims of unfairness, that real justice develops
character within us.

Lord, your justice is always good and right.

Proverbs 28: 13

*He who conceals his sins does not prosper, but
whoever confesses and renounces them finds
mercy.*

The fact that we covered our sin kept us hopelessly
addicted/codependent. Part of our denial system
involved covering up, excusing, minimizing, or rationalizing. At last, when we could no longer escape the reality that we were in trouble, we
admitted to our addiction/codependency. Admitting was only the First Step, but slowly we were
able not only to admit but also to see we were powerless to change.

As we grow in our understanding of the Twelve
Steps, we begin the moral inventory and finally
through confession to self, God, and another person we find God's mercy and forgiveness. The
decks are now cleared from the debris of the past,
and our new life of sobriety can prosper. The God of
recovery has great things for us, but first the rubble
from our addiction/codependency must be removed, then he can begin to build. Those things we
covered grew, but when we brought them out into
the light of God's mercy and forgiveness, their
power over our lives was greatly reduced. That
which once caused shame can become the very
place that we touch others' lives. Our greatest weakness before recovery can become our greatest
strength in recovery.

*Father, give me courage to confess and
renounce my sins.*

Proverbs 28: 14

Blessed is the man who always fears the Lord,
but he who hardens his heart falls into trouble.

Addiction/codependency causes our hearts to become hardened. We feel so awful about ourselves that we assume God is angry with us—after all, everyone else seems to be. Our addiction/codependency numbs our emotions and controls our wills, thus the hardening begins. Without a sensitive, feeling heart, the conscience becomes seared, and it is easy to fall into trouble.

Recovery and the wisdom of the Twelve Steps begin to awaken our senses. Our consciences keep us out of trouble, often before we have actually strayed from the path.

Our intimate relationship with the Lord is a source of strength as well as peace. The more we learn about the Lord, the more we can develop deeper trust and allow him to soften our hearts. He gives a heart of flesh in exchange for the old stony heart. To feel can be a source of pain, especially when our consciences bother us, but to not feel is far more dangerous. The pain of a hot stove causes us to remove our hands quickly; not to feel the heat would result in serious burns. Likewise, to feel the guilt helps us repent or keeps us from doing the wrong that could leave us with scars for a lifetime.

O God, help me feel the conviction that will keep me
from trouble.

Proverbs 28: 23

He who rebukes a man will in the end gain more
favor than he who has a flattering tongue.

Recovery requires honesty and our willingness to
be open to correction. Those we welcome into our
lives as sponsors or close recovering friends are the
ones from whom we need to hear the truth. A
searching, fearless inventory sounds like the removal of our defense mechanisms and our denial
systems and looking squarely into the messes we
have created. Often when someone begins to rebuke, it is easy to become defensive. Our feelings
hurt; we may feel anger and we may possibly want
to lash back. But that will not help us to recover.

We must be willing to hear the rebuke. To remind
ourselves that this person genuinely cares about us
helps to ease the sting. Our old addictive/codepen-
dent nature greatly desires someone who will be on
our side and will agree with us and flatter us, but
that will feed the addiction/codependency. To recover we must be willing to accept the constructive
criticism of those who know us best, even when we
want to stop up our ears.

Father, please send people who will rebuke me
when I need it.

Proverbs 28: 25

*A greedy man stirs up dissension, but he who
trusts in the Lord will prosper.*

The proverbs remind us often to trust in the Lord.
In those few words Solomon stated the Second and
Third Steps of our recovery. Only as we are able to
trust him can we experience serenity and peace of
mind. If we are convinced that he can handle our
present situation, we can turn it over to him. Being
the strong-willed children that we are, we try to
control things for as long as we can. Sometimes it
takes a crisis to convince us of our limitations, and
we must trust the Lord to work it out.

What wisdom we have attained when we are
aware that those two Steps work on more than our
addiction/codependency. We have learned the secret of trusting the Lord in every area of our lives.
The more we trust, the more we find ourselves re-
laxing in his tender care. The more we turn our
lives over to him, the more peace we experience.
This is true prosperity.

*O God, you have prospered me in so many ways as I
have learned how to trust you.*

Proverbs 28: 26

He who trusts in himself is a fool, but he who walks in wisdom is kept safe.

Wisdom is knowledge that we have learned how to use to make life work. Usually through pain, our knowledge has become wisdom. Knowledge has a tendency to encourage us to trust in self. Wisdom knows that no one but God can keep us safe; therefore wisdom depends completely on the Lord. Wisdom is more mature than knowledge and knows how to wait in peace while God works it out. Trusting in self keeps us in trouble. Often we fail to yield our will because we think we know the way or the solution. The greatest wisdom we have is knowing that we must depend upon God for our recovery, for the changes within, for the grace and mercy to continue on difficult days, for the courage to face ourselves. He is the author and finisher of our recovery. It is he who made us, and not we ourselves. He knows us better than anyone else does, including ourselves, and he knows how to bring us through the present circumstance. To trust that knowledge is wisdom.

Lord, help me walk in wisdom and trust you.

Proverbs 28: 27

He who gives to the poor will lack nothing, but he who closes his eyes to them receives many curses.

Taking the hope of recovery to others who are struggling is one of the strong points in recovery. What we give away we keep forever, what we hoard slips through our fingers and is lost forever. The hurting people who are still bound by addiction/codependency are those who need our message of hope. To feed the physically hungry is important, but we also need to feed those who are hungry for hope. As we share the message of Twelve-Step recovery and the possibilities of healing for others, we are ensuring our recovery. Many people work the first eleven Steps; but recovery is a Twelve-Step program, and to omit the last Step sets us up to stumble. To reach out of our secure group and invite someone who isn't quite as fortunate is one way to give to the poor. To invest time listening to someone and to sponsor them in their recovery is a way to give to the poor. To share our own personal story with others is a way of giving to the poor. As we bless those around us, we are blessed.

Father, make me sensitive to those who are needy around me.

Proverbs 29: 1

A man who remains stiff-necked after many
rebukes will suddenly be destroyed—without
remedy.

Many of us who are today enjoying the fruits of recovery and a sober life-style once knew the darkness of hitting bottom. Many addicts/codependents
must experience the loss of something important
before we turn to the Twelve Steps. We may have
faced many trials and many speeches by those who
tried to help us see what our addiction/codepen-
dency was doing to us and those around us. We
may have tried for a while to straighten out our
lives, to no avail. The more people tried to help us
see the error of our ways, the more resentful we
may have become, hardening our hearts.

But the way of addiction/codependency is always a downward road to destruction. It was God's
severe mercy to let us experience the bottom, because few of us ever felt powerless enough to seek
recovery until we faced that severe disappointment
or loss. The wonderful thing is that our bottom
brought us into the life-style of recovery, a way of
hope, healing, and happiness.

Lord, thank you for softening my hard heart and
making my neck movable again by
allowing me to hit bottom.

Proverbs 29: 6

An evil man is snared by his own sin, but a
righteous one can sing and be glad.

The contrast of before and after recovery began is
obvious to those of us who are living it. Over and
over we were snared by our addiction/codepen-
dency and brought into deeper bondage. It seemed
the more we struggled, the tighter our chains became. There was no song, only anguished groans
from the depths of our being.

Today, after recovery has progressed a bit, we
are free and happy. Even in the difficult times we
know the song of freedom, and we rejoice in the fact
that we are no longer merely existing but now really living. Recovery is actually that. The program
helps us to recover that which the enemy of addic-
tion/codependency had stolen. The maturer our
recovery becomes, the more we awaken to true life.
Our eyes are open. We see the beauty of life not just
with our physical eyes but with our hearts. Our ears
hear, but not our ears only; our souls hear the song
of recovery and join in the glad song of freedom.

Father, you have turned my slavery into freedom, and I
sing with my entire being, I'm free, I'm free!

Proverbs 29: 11

A fool gives full vent to his anger, but a wise man keeps himself under control.

Anger is one of the more difficult emotions for recovering people to process correctly. To explode injures others; to repress anger hurts ourselves. Anger is deadly and will sabotage our recovery unless we learn how to handle it appropriately. A fool could be considered as one who is unlearned or uneducated, and when we were unlearned or uneducated, we were foolish in the ways we handled our angry feelings. Some of us put a top on the anger and held onto it; others blew our tops and vented it all.

The wisdom of recovery tells us to turn to God with whatever we are powerless over and give it to him. We are taught the secret of one day at a time, keeping things simple, forgiving and making amends when we have hurt someone else. We are only under control when we have given control over to God; any other time we are at risk. Recovery teaches us the importance of turning ourselves over to the care of God and allowing him to receive our anger until we have learned enough coping skills to defuse our anger in a healthy manner.

Lord, I give you my angry feelings. Will you teach me how to deal with them?

Proverbs 29: 15

*The rod of correction imparts wisdom, but a child
left to himself disgraces his mother.*

The rod of correction seems like a strange way to
obtain wisdom, and yet Solomon tells us that we
learn wisdom by the rod of correction. The entire
Twelve-Step program is correction for our wrong
ways, habits, and attitudes about living. Our sponsors and other recovering friends become rods of
correction as they confront us with denial or avoidance or stinking thinking. Many times the consequences of our folly become the rods through
which we are corrected and trained. Restitution and
making amends is another way of training us and
giving us wisdom. When we are left to ourselves,
we will always make a mess and bring disgrace to
ourselves.

Correction from someone who loves us, whether
God or a friend, is one example of tough love, and
we must have those people in our lives if we are to
recover. It is never God's anger or rejection of us
that brings his rod of correction but his love and
concern for our lives. It may be difficult for us to
understand the rod of correction being love, but
nevertheless it is God's love for us. Recovery is the
result of accepting the correction with a willing
heart.

Lord, lay the rod on me when I need to be corrected.

Proverbs 29: 18

Where there is no revelation, the people cast off restraint; but blessed is he who keeps the law.

Before recovery we had no revelation of the plan of recovery or the Twelve Steps, and we had absolutely no restraint in our lives. We wanted to be free, but in our diseased concept of freedom, we got into bondage. As we grow in our knowledge of the Twelve Steps, we receive revelation of what true freedom is, and we realize that true freedom is found in keeping certain laws and abiding under certain restrictions. Wisdom teaches us through the Twelve Steps that to maintain serenity we must follow guidelines. As we learn to live in the framework of the Twelve Steps, our lives and relationships are blessed. To follow the structure of the Twelve Steps brings us into true freedom.

Between the beginning of recovery and the maturity of recovery are worlds of things to learn, and each step between is a step solidifying and stabilizing our life-changing revelation. Things that we once rebelled against we now appreciate and consider important. Law becomes not something that hampers and impedes our life but that protects and enhances our life-style of recovery.

God, thank you for the revelation that helps me appreciate the laws.

Proverbs 29: 19

A servant cannot be corrected by mere words;
though he understands, he will not respond.

Sometimes we need more than words to teach us, and sometimes lessons in recovery are better learned by demonstration rather than by speech. Anyone can talk about the Twelve Steps, anyone can read the Steps, but a life changed by living the Steps is always more effective. Words are powerful, no doubt about it, but a living testimony is so much more dramatic. We are often moved by the lives of those who have accomplished recovery rather than by the words and theories of those who talk about it. Sponsors are those who do more than just point the way for us; they are willing to walk with us on difficult days because they know that we need more than just words, we need someone who has been there and someone who remembers how it feels to struggle.

We then are able to mature in recovery as we actively practice the Steps in all of our affairs. Every area of our lives is enhanced by the wisdom of recovery. We then become a living testimony for those who follow behind us, not merely pointing the way but walking them through the hard times and encouraging them with our presence.

O God, thank you for those who have practiced what
they preach about recovery.

Proverbs 29: 25

Fear of man will prove to be a snare, but whoever trusts in the Lord is kept safe.

Solomon gives us another clearly defined before and after picture of recovery. Before we entered recovery we may have been fearful of people. In an unhealthy way, we concerned ourselves with what they thought about us, what they said about us, and we became entangled in trying to control others' lives. We became ensnared by trying to make people think a certain way about us. Fearing man will keep us in bondage. To be afraid of a person's ability to harm us is one kind of fear, but to be afraid that a person doesn't think well of us can be easier to fall into.

The Twelve Steps begin to teach us to depend completely on God for everything. When we were fearful of people, we tried to control. When we trust in the Lord, we learn to let go and let God be in control. Peace is the result. We cannot control life, emotions, others, or self. To try to do so is both futile and frustrating. We cannot make others think well of us, like us, or approve of us. We are powerless over that area of our lives. We learn to rest in the Lord and rely upon him, and we experience serenity.

Father, help me to trust you when I want to control others' opinions about me.

Proverbs 30: 5

Every word of God is flawless; he is a shield to those who take refuge in him.

The God of recovery shields us from every circumstance and situation that would hinder our recovery. The more we run to him, the more we learn to trust his wisdom, his protection. Much of our recovery is simply learning to become dependent on God rather than self-reliant, and the result is recovery and victory. As we come to know his Word, his direction is clearly seen and understood in each situation. This is the wisdom needed for consistent recovery.

God's ways are never our ways, but his methods are perfect. He knows what we need as individuals, and he doesn't try to force us into a mold that doesn't fit. Our plan of recovery is one of a kind, made to fit our personality, and guaranteed to work in our lives.

The longer we walk the road of recovery, the deeper our trust in God. The more we trust him, the more secure we are in his love and acceptance. Our first ability to trust was very childlike. We knew he could free us from addiction/codependency. But the wisdom of recovery teaches us that he can be trusted for far more than freedom from addiction/codependency. He can be trusted for every day of our lives.

Father, thank you for teaching me to take refuge in you.

Proverbs 30: 7–9

Two things I ask of you, O Lord; do not refuse me before I die: Keep falsehood and lies far from me; give me neither poverty nor riches, but give me only my daily bread. Otherwise, I may have too much and disown you and say, "Who is the Lord?" Or I may become poor and steal, and so dishonor the name of my God.

The wisdom of recovery teaches us a life well balanced in every area. Proverbs reminds us of that principle again in this passage. Extremes always bring us into some kind of bondage. When we have too much, we are out of balance. When we don't have enough, we are out of balance. Being the humans we are, we always take matters into our own hands and then leave the God of recovery out of our lives. Temperance, balance, or disciplined living is the theme of recovery. Total dependence on the God of recovery is necessary for our maturity in recovery. Yet one of the first signs of relapse is when we begin to rely on ourselves again. We try to solve the problems we face with our natural understanding, human knowledge, and ability, and when we do, we get into trouble. Solomon knew the tendency of humans to try to be in control and how easily we resort to the carnal part of ourselves for solutions to our problems; and then he prayed, "Lord just keep me in balance."

O Lord, thank you for the balance that recovery has brought into my life.

Proverbs 30: 15

*"The leech has two daughters. 'Give! Give!'
they cry."*

Solomon is a master at defining situations and confronting issues. Here he describes for us the persons who refuse to do their part in recovery. There are those who take the First Step to mean that they aren't responsible for anything and they therefore depend on everyone else to do the work. If we fall into this category of people in recovery, we will never get well. Recovery is a partnership, and everyone has a part to accomplish. God always does his part, but do we always do ours? The person that Solomon describes here expects everyone else to give, and if recovery doesn't happen easily, the journey becomes someone else's responsibility. When it's time to walk, this person demands to ride or to be carried in someone's arms. If the mountain is steep or if the valley is deep, someone else has to do the work. Needless to say, this person will not recover because the concept of recovery has not yet been understood. We are powerless over addiction/codependency, yet we are responsible to turn our lives and wills over to God, and we are responsible for taking the Steps of recovery.

God, teach me to know my part in recovery.

Proverbs 30: 32–33

*If you have played the fool and exalted yourself,
or if you have planned evil, clap your hand over
your mouth! For as churning the milk produces
butter, and as twisting the nose produces blood,
so stirring up anger produces strife.*

We have learned that recovery involves more than
just the Twelve Steps and our addiction/codependency. Sober living affects every aspect of our lives.
One of the areas we struggle against in recovery is
that part within us that wants to be exalted. We
would never say outright that we want to be above
anyone else, yet every argument, every angry outburst, every silent treatment declares that we think
we are right, our way is best, and we want the other
person to agree with us. Pride is possibly one of the
last areas to recover because it requires dying to our
selfish ambition. Solomon says that we are fools
when we try to exalt ourselves, that it is as painful
to others as twisting the nose and making it bleed.

As we mature in our concept of recovery, we become more willing to yield to others. We learn to let
some of the anger go. We realize that others do have
opinions that differ from ours. We learn to live and
let live. Learning to accept others' differences and
learning the humility of asking forgiveness bring
us into the freedom we've sought for so long.

*Father, sometimes I forget that it's OK for someone to
have a different opinion. Please help me.*

The Twelve Steps of Alcoholics Anonymous

1. We admitted we were powerless over alcohol—that our lives had become unmanageable.

2. Came to believe that a Power greater than ourselves could restore us to sanity.

3. Made a decision to turn our will and our lives over to the care of God *as we understood Him.*

4. Made a searching and fearless moral inventory of ourselves.

5. Admitted to God, to ourselves, and to another human being the exact nature of our wrongs.

6. Were entirely ready to have God remove all these defects of character.

7. Humbly asked Him to remove our shortcomings.

8. Made a list of all persons we had harmed, and became willing to make amends to them all.

9. Made direct amends to such people wherever possible, except when to do so would injure them or others.

10. Continued to take personal inventory and when we were wrong promptly admitted it.

11. Sought through prayer and meditation to improve our conscious contact with God, *as we understood Him,* praying only for knowledge of God's will for us and the power to carry that out.

12. Having had a spiritual awakening as the result of these steps, we tried to carry this message to alcoholics, and to practice these principles in all our affairs.